"Funny, heart-centered and raw. Finally,
connect to!"

　　　　　　　　- Jennifer Ho, Founder/CEO of Hangar Studios

"Tonia is the wise messenger of an amazing spiritual and practical
blueprint to transform outmoded beliefs and practices about money
into a joyful journey to abundance. I love this book."

　　　　　　　　- Tami Coyne, Spiritual Coach-Counselor and
　　　　　　　　Author of *Your Life's Work* and
　　　　　　　Co-Author of *The Spiritual Chicks Question Everything*

"Tonia is the archetypal Money Whisperer! In this book she takes you
by the hand and guides you through a process where you can't help but
transform your own relationship with money. What I love about Tonia
is that she combines the spiritual with the super-practical and delivers
a step-by-step approach that meets you wherever you're at right now.
Buying this book is surely the most potent investment you could make
in yourself right now!"

　　　　　　　　- Nicola Humber, Author of *Heal Your Inner Good Girl*,
　　　　　　　　UNBOUND and *Unbound Writing*

"By tapping into years of financial experiences, and by taking a step
back to truly understand the relationship between money and
power, Tonia unveils her unique process to achieving financial freedom
and happiness."

　　　　　　　　- Anthony W. Pulice, CPA CFE

"Permission to be Rich achieves the impossible – it heals your emotional blocks with money and builds a new and satisfying relationship
with abundance – a must read."

　　　　　　　　- Linda Joyce, Author, Astrologer & Life Coach

"Growing up as a child of The Depression, I have experienced first-hand how hard it is to give yourself permission to enjoy abundance. Tonia cracks the code on how to just that with her authentic style and enthusiastic prose."

- Audrey Schwartz, Financial Planner

Authentic - Genuine - Inspirational. Permission to be Rich is a gift of wisdom. Tonia brilliantly unveils her raw journey of navigating the relationship between money and life. She provides a clear blueprint for financial freedom and how to gain control over one's relationship with money, while having fun and enjoying all the joy life has to offer.

- Adam Gonzalez, Ph.D.

"Tonia's approach is to take the fear out of finance and to help you discover the joy (yes, the joy!) in balancing your books. I don't call her The Money Whisperer for nothing."

- Mark Connolly, Spiritual Alchemist

In Permission to Be Rich, Tonia reminds us that power lies not with money itself (or how much of it we have) but with the person who holds it. While Tonia has had some amazing experiences which led to incredible insights, she breaks down her teachings into digestible, logical and enjoyable pieces for the rest of us! She is the guide and cheerleader I did not know I needed, but was so glad I had, on this money journey!

- Gina Scarpa, Attorney and Executive Coach

"A woman's relationship to money and wealth is one of the most important pieces to our capacity to heal the world. Tonia takes all the lies we've been taught about money and alchemizes them into new ways of using, spending, and receiving wealth as women leaders. Read this book and give yourself - finally - permission to be rich."

-Megan Jo Wilson, Coach, Business Mentor, Author of *No More Playing Small*

PERMISSION
to be
RICH

5 Steps to Become
More Powerful Than Money

Tonia Gaudiuso

Paperback 978-1-913590-35-2
Ebook 978-1-913590-36-9

The Unbound Press
www.theunboundpress.com

Hey unbound one!

Welcome to this magical book brought to you by The Unbound Press.

At The Unbound Press we believe that when women write freely from the fullest expression of who they are, it can't help but activate a feeling of deep connection and transformation in others. When we come together, we become more and we're changing the world, one book at a time!

This book has been carefully crafted by both the author and publisher with the intention of inspiring you to move ever more deeply into who you truly are.

We hope that this book helps you to connect with your Unbound Self and that you feel called to pass it on to others who want to live a more fully expressed life.

With much love,
Nicola Humber

Founder of The Unbound Press
www.theunboundpress.com

For Sante Scorcia

CONTENTS

A Message to My Reader

As we start this journey together, it's important to me to communicate with you that all I am sharing, teaching and writing is not just a concept or something I'm regurgitating from books I've read. Everything I've learned is because I was courageous enough to take the knowledge from books on money, abundance, wealth, and prosperity and put them into practice. What you're getting is the blueprint based on the daily actions and habits I created from my collective experiences of joy, pain, heartbreak, shame, excitement, bliss, guilt, success, vulnerability (and whatever other emotion there is!) so that the journey is easier for you, less confusing to digest, and to comfort you in knowing that you're not alone in your experiences with money. When you invite awareness into your life, you are choosing to release the emotions, thoughts, habits and beliefs that are no longer serving you. My intention is to teach you my money system so that you feel empowered when you approach money instead of feeling shame or being overly harsh with yourself. This is a process that took me seven years to create and will be known to you by the end of this book.

So, get ready for an adventure of play, discovery, vulnerability and transformation. Let me awaken you to the joy and freedom of life that doesn't cost a thing. Through storytelling, I share my own money pain and make unveiling the illusion of money fun. I reveal my money humility, and how I mastered flipping the script of my life into a divine comedy. I was put on this path to introduce you to a new money paradigm, to guide you towards a healthy and harmonious relationship with money. A perspective that connects money to being an expression of love and gratitude with an inner conviction that money is a tool and way for you to say "thank you." By reading this book, you are activating a mindset of appreciation for the new commodities of this world: love, people, connection, health, touch, quality time, nature, wellbeing, kindness, laughter, happiness, joy, space and everything else that comes free – but until now, you've overlooked it precisely because it's free.

This book is for the money underdog. Financial equality begins with us empowering our minds to know, unequivocally, that we are entitled to the riches of this universe. In this book, I'm going to provide you with a set of tools and technical guidance to help you master your daily finances. It starts with us taking control back from money and embracing an abundant mindset, then protecting that mindset like a ninja! The power of one is mighty, but when we join forces, the power of the masses is an unstoppable force. The mission is financial liberation. I'm calling on all humans who want a richer soul life and for the money in their bank accounts to reflect their soul's richness. It's time for a revolution. A money revolution, and all are welcome to join.

Introduction

Through my experiences of working with people as a professional and financial organizer, I have accumulated a lot of money wisdom that wants to be shared with the world. I am a financial intuitive, here to restore the integrity of money and abundance, to remove the illusion of money, the power it holds, and bring it back to the true source of its power: us. People. You and me. I am here to teach you that money need not be a scary thing. Money has historically been used to manipulate, but it doesn't need to be that way. Money is a tool, just like a car or a bike. It is a form of currency and its real purpose is gratitude.

The world we live in uses money as a way to control and limit what we are able to do. A way to clip our wings. It has us choosing from our wallets versus our hearts. "Sure, this sounds all well and good," I hear you say, "but how is money being an expression of love and gratitude going to support me if I can't pay my rent? What about my mortgage? Taxes? Student loans? What about all of that?"

Well, that's why I wrote this book. To address it by teaching you the tools to manage your finances and restore a healthy foundation for your money.

In this world, you've been taught to put your energy and focus on what's missing versus all that you have. It's your perspective that holds the power by choosing where and what you put your energy and focus into. Are you choosing scarcity or abundance? The current foundation is based on scarcity. This lack mindset has led to the raping of our planet of her natural resources because we want more, yet, we have more than enough. We are in a world that promotes materialism and seeking outward things for inside happiness. On a daily basis, we are all wasteful in some form: with food, clothing, furniture and so much more. This is wrong. This is not what creates happiness. Things do not create happiness; it's just an illusion, and today I am here to wake you up, dear reader, to this very illusion.

Picking up this book was your inner call to say that it is now time to restore yourself to your natural state of abundance. If we are breathing, we are worthy of it. It's time to activate ourselves as the creators we are. It's time to write our stories and start using money as the tool it is. A tool to say "thank you" for the things we purchase and the ways in which we give it. To recognize that money is only a currency and only one form of currency. Money is not magic, power or happiness. We are the magic, we are the power, we create our own happiness and we can empower ourselves to see and use money in a new light.

Before we get started, I would like to share the reading journey you will go on and what the best way is for you to tackle all the juicy goodness you will receive in this book. In Part One (Money and Me), I'll share my money journey – complete with all the ups and downs that ultimately revealed money's methodology to me. This way, you can understand how I became a financial intuitive and money whisperer, and hopefully it will answer your question of "Why the F should I listen to this chick?!"

In Part Two (Five F's to Financial Freedom), you will journey through the five stages of money: Focus, Foundation, Freedom, Flow and Fun. The worksheets in these stages guide you along the process of creating a new money system for yourself. Within this book are sample worksheets to illustrate actions to take. You can find the blank worksheets as PDF files on my website (**www.toniag.com/rich-resources**). My entire money methodology and the tools I use to work with my clients are in Part Two of this book. Take your time reading it so that you digest all the information.

In this part you will also find my personal journal entries and intimacies with money. These are my mini money life lessons where at times I expose my own painful challenges with money. This will help you know that you are not alone in this pain. At the end of the book, there are blank pages for you to use at any time to write questions, notes or maybe your own money vulnerabilities. Consider these your money magic pages – have fun with them!

Throughout the book, I'll be using the word "universe" to refer to the concepts of Source, Spirit, God, Goddess, humanity, energy and oneness, to name but a few. Whilst you're reading, feel free to replace "universe" with a word that you feel represents your higher self or a powerful energy. Let the adventure begin with the story of Money and Me.

> **FUN TIP:** If you find you work better in collaboration with others, you can create your own money magic mastermind to read this book with and complete the worksheets in Part Two.

Part One:
Money and Me

"Life is either a daring adventure, or nothing.
To keep our faces toward change & behave like free spirits
in the presence of fate is strength undefeatable."

- Helen Keller

Chapter 1: Love

As I look back on my life, I realize that I have had a lifelong, passionate romance with …money! Money has always spoken to me and I've always found it to be so much fun. It began when I was a little girl, five years old to be exact. I went to dance school and lived for the recitals: the makeup, costumes, performing in front of an audience – those things were all just heaven to me. At the recitals, my family could spot me easily: they would just look for the least graceful girl on stage and there I was! I've never been the delicate type and my dancing style certainly reflected that.

There's one recital that stands out from them all. My family would always remind me about it because I was super annoying, going around the house singing and doing that one performance all the time, as loudly as possible! At the recital, I'm wearing a red and white candy-striped leotard, complete with white leggings and a red headband with red feathers sticking out of it. The song we're performing to is "Diamonds are a Girl's Best Friend" by Marilyn Monroe and I was totally in LOVE with this message.

Now, I can't tell you what all the moves were or remember much of the recital itself. I just remember, vividly, the feeling of absolute joy when doing this one move where we put our hands out in front of us, in beautiful white silk gloves, showing off the diamonds on our hands as we sang the words to the song and shook our hips to the beat.

To this day I still love getting dressed up and shaking my hips! From an early age, I was hooked on the materialistic side of money. I fell head over heels in love with it. There are many moments in my childhood that reveal my love for money and all that it could buy me. In the third grade, I wrote the following story expressing my love of jewels and things.

What I Would Find in My Pot of Gold

"In my pot of gold, I would like to find a car so I can drive and so I don't have to waste any money. I would like to find $99,223 dollars so I can get a lot of things. There's just one more thing I want and that is lots of jewelry. What I would do with this is bring it over the rainbow to the world and I can use the car there and the money and the jewelry."

Yep, I believed in Leprechauns and rainbows with a pot of gold at the end. My oh my, was I in trouble and forming quite a materialistic connection to money from early on. When I found this story, what made me laugh is the obscure number of $99,223. Really? Where did that come from? One thing is for certain, I'm definitely unique in my thinking!

Fast forward to my Barbie period. Sure, I owned some – but they became secondary when I discovered the joy of accompanying my Mom to the bank and the thrill of creating my own laminated credit cards from the beautiful, shiny pamphlets. Yep, you heard me right: credit cards. Back in the day when I was growing up, electronic applications did not exist, so instead there were these beautiful pamphlets with images of the gold American Express card, and you had to manually fill out these paper applications in order to apply for a credit card. It's not applying for the credit card that interested me, it was the oh-so-real image of the credit card. I would take these pamphlets home with me and turn them into an arts and crafts project. I would cut out the credit card picture, measure it out against a piece of cardboard, cut out the cardboard and place it behind the image to make it strong, before adding the final touch by laminating it.

What would I do with these laminated cards? I would put them in my wallet, of course. Not only in my personal wallet, but in the extra wallets I had, too. That way, when I played "office" with my friends, we all had proper wallets like adults. So, while other kids were at home playing with their Barbie, I was at home organizing wallets for my friends so we could play "working at the office" in my basement. Yep, office!! I couldn't wait to be an adult and be the boss some day and make money. The seeds of having my own business were planted early on in my mind. I had a whole outfit that was my "executive work outfit." Power came in the form of high heels and a blazer.

My relationship with money continued to grow in curious ways. Besides playing office, I loved playing with cash registers. I was (and still am) ridiculously obsessed with cash registers! I just love them. I love what they are all about. The buttons: the feel of those buttons when you push them down, the sound the cash register makes when it opens … I freaking love it. Back when I was in elementary school, one of my friends had a real cash register at her house. Every day after school, I was by her house playing "store" and using that cash register. I couldn't get enough of it! What did I expect, it's one of the traditional homes for money − of course I would love it!

My "executive work outfits" and practicing my, I'm not playing face.

Chapter 2: Power

I was about twelve years old when I learned to manipulate money to get what I want. It all began with my mom saying "no" to my request for a new pair of sneakers. At that time in my life, I was playing basketball and I was good at it, Most Valuable Player (MVP) on my team good. I was at the top of my game (yep, at twelve), and everyone else on the team had great name brand sneakers like Nikes and Jordans. There I was, Ms. MVP with my Champion sneakers.

One time, at the height of my twelve-year-old basketball career, my mom and I went to the sneaker store on Coney Island Avenue to get a new pair. We would go to this one particular store because, as my mom put it, *"They had fabulous prices."* I had the expectation of getting Nikes or Jordans just like everyone else. I gathered up the courage and asked my mom if I could have cool sneakers. She responded with the golden question of most immigrant parents: *"How much?"* The conversation went something a little like this:

> **Me**: *"Mom, can I have these sneakers?"* (pointing at the pair I had in mind)

> **Mom**: *"What's the difference between those sneakers and the sneakers I have in my hand?"*

> **Me**: *(I say nothing and shrug my shoulders)*

Mom: *"Is the rubber underneath the same?"*

Me: *(reluctantly) "Yes."*

Mom: *"The material of the sneakers is the same?"*

Me: *(sensing where this is going) "Yes."*

Mom: *"So, the only difference is the name?"*

Me: *"Yes"*

Mom: *(decisively) "Absolutely not! The sneakers I'm holding are absolutely perfect and I'm not paying more for something just because of the name!"*

I felt defeated and embarrassed. I wanted to fit in with my team and have the cool name-brand shoes. Me and my materialistic self. My mom was right, but I didn't see it that way at the time. I certainly did not do well at hearing "no." As a result, I learned to start making money for myself so that no-one could say no to me anymore. At age thirteen, I started babysitting with my cousin and making $10 an hour. I was making my own money. No, I didn't rush out to buy myself the Jordans right there and then, but this did start me off on a track of believing that money equals independence. I would take this mindset all the way to twenty-nine years old.

Fast-forward to me at sixteen years old: I was still madly in love with money and even more with making it and the freedom it brought. Our relationship matured and this love of money brought me to my first official job working at Olympian Bank in Bayridge, Brooklyn. This relationship is also what had me stop playing basketball in High School and not try out for the Varsity team. I knew the commitment it required and I couldn't work and play basketball. I chose money instead of joy (lesson learned).

Twice a month, I would work with my best friend, Kristine, and we would stuff envelopes with customers' bank statements (back then there was no electronic banking or debit cards, it was the good ol' check writing days), and on the first and fifteenth of the month, depending on if they were personal or business bank statements, they had to be mailed out. I was getting paid $12 an hour to do this while sitting next to my best friend. Life was grand!

I was self-righteous and I had money. I could go to the city, go shopping, hang out with my friends, and no one could question me. I thanked money for all of it. My parents made it clear from an early age that they would only pay for the essentials: food, shelter, clothing (I went to Catholic school so I always had to wear a uniform) and school. Everything else was up to me to get or wait for my birthday or Christmas when gifts were given. I thank God for this mentality because it taught me to earn for myself. I learned what it feels like to be responsible for what I want and then going out and getting it. Working hard does pay off. This hunger for more got Kristine and I promoted to encoding checks at the bank. This is how the bank knew what checks were being deposited and computed it into your bank account. Now, by this you can tell I was really in the home of money and learning about the institutions it belonged to!

Then, something happened. The bank was closing because they were merging with another. So, what did that mean? It meant a severance package for me and I got to collect Unemployment Insurance Benefits because I was laid off. My severance package gave me enough to take myself away to Cancun and enjoy the summer before starting college. I just kept attracting the money I wanted and at the perfect time.

Chapter 3: Pleases Me

By now, I'm a freshmen student at Pace University and living my life to the fullest. My friend Josephine got an internship working in the accounting department at Seabury and Smith. She referred me to her boss, I got an interview, and I'm hired right there and then on the spot. I'm going clubbing with my friends in the city and spending my weekends away in the Hamptons, Atlantic City and Hunter Mountain. There were also the Spring break vacations on top of this, and I had the money to do it all. Oh, and I was saving money at the same time, too! My love for money always seemed to bring me to my next opportunity.

My luck was always just that way with money and work. I wanted it, I got it and I worked hard for it. Seabury and Smith was on the forty-ninth floor of the World Trade Center, Building Two. I thought I was such hot stuff working in one of the iconic World Trade Center buildings. As you now know, since I was a young girl, all I wanted was to work in an office in a corporate environment. This was the perfect start to me being that high-powered executive. My plan was working. I was getting my degree in Business Management with a minor in Psychology. I believed that these two subjects went hand in hand. I figured that in business, it's beneficial to know how people operate and think.

At that point, I was in money-making mode and ready to receive information on becoming successful. There was one professor who had a great impact on me because he had his own business and was teaching as a way to "pay it forward" in his life for all the success he had enjoyed. This resonated with me because he was teaching from life experience, not just from the pages of a book. On the first day of class, he told us about Individual Retirement Accounts (IRA). He said that if there was one thing we were going to listen to and take away from his class, he hoped that this was it. He explained that if we invested in an IRA at this age, for seven consecutive years, depositing two thousand dollars a year in this IRA, at a growth rate of ten percent on our investment and if we did not contribute any more money to this ever again, that we could retire with one million dollars in the bank (the link to the article, "Rich Man, Poor Man" can be found in the back of the book in the resource's section). Imagine knowing at 25 years old your retirement is set up for $1,000,000 and it only cost you $14,000. This is compounding interest at work for you. Now imagine parents doing this for their kids instead of buying them things and parties. Just saying!

Now, this totally blew my mind! Of course, I didn't start investing at that moment like he suggested, but I did when I was twenty-one. I am still reaping the benefits from this advice, knowing I have money for when I retire no matter where I work. I read all the books from the recommended reading list he gave us. After reading the book on Mary Kay, More Than a Pink Cadillac, and Coach K's book, Leading With The Heart, I knew I was going to be a leader, a Chief Executive Officer (CEO) and run a heart-centered business. In other words, I would be doing things differently.

Chapter 4: Deceives Me

At this stage, I'm now in the corporate world and it's here I learn about the control money has over people, over me, and the ways in which corporations use that control to their advantage. 9/11 was the event that made me see that, and it altered my childhood dream of world domination in the corporate world and being a CEO. I'm nineteen years old, it's the beginning of Sophomore year and I am on the train to Pace University for my 9:00 a.m. History class. The train stopped at Rector Street and it didn't start moving again. It just so happened that my friend Josephine (who was in the same History class and worked with me in the World Trade Center) ended up on the same train, in the same subway car. We stayed in our seats during the train ride because we were both doing the reading for our class. When the train stopped, I went over to ask her if she wanted to walk to class because I didn't want to be late. It was almost 9:00 a.m., and the walk took at least five to ten minutes. I knew this because I did this walk during my lunch break at the World Trade Center. I still love going for walks and exploring the city, it's a simple act that brings me such joy. Anyway, we decided we did not want to be late and so started walking.

We headed out of the subway and as we did, I saw bits of paper flying around in the sky. I asked Josephine, "*Is there a ticker tape parade going on that we don't know about?*" Oh, how innocent I was. We continued walking and within a couple of minutes, we found out what was really happening. A plane hit into the World Trade Center at 8:46 a.m. and that was what caused our train to stop. There we were, standing outside of World Trade Center One, staring at a gaping hole on the side of the building. Debris was falling from the buildings, but a man standing next to me confirmed it was not actually debris falling at all: it was people jumping out of the top of the building. Horror in the making. Innocence gone. At 9:03 a.m., about five minutes later, I heard this huge explosion happen above my head. I looked up and all I could see was red. It was the second plane hitting World Trade Center Two. Suddenly, it was like the running of the bulls – except it wasn't bulls, and I wasn't in Spain.

Everyone scurried from the buildings. Josephine and I started running, in shock at what we just saw and not understanding what we just experienced. As we were running, Josephine fell down and asked me to leave her because she couldn't go on. She couldn't breathe and was having a panic attack. I grabbed her, lifted her up and we ran together. We ran into a deli by school where I got Josephine some water. It was here that we saw on the TV the two buildings on fire with the headlines "TERRORIST ATTACK." We continued walking to school, which was only a block away. I ran in in a frenzy and grabbed the first landline phone I could see off an administrator's desk as she looked at me like I was nuts. I told her to go look outside without batting an eyelid. I continued to dial the number for my mom because cell phones weren't working. Once I got on the phone with my mom I started crying. I asked if I needed to go to class and she urged me to do what felt right for me. No one could imagine that the buildings were going to fall. I'm not sure if I realized at this moment that this event would change the course of my life – and the lives of so many others – forever.

I then walked out of school and saw two of my best friends sitting outside on the steps, Lisa and Chris. I explained to them all I had just seen, teared up, and said we needed to get the hell out of the city. A group of us started to gather and some wanted to take a taxi or a subway home. Adamantly, I said, "*We are leaving now and walking over that bridge*" (pointing to the Brooklyn Bridge). As we were walking over the Brooklyn Bridge, I heard this terrible rumbling sound. I turned and saw the World Trade Center crumble and implode like a scene from an action movie. I thought that everyone on the forty-ninth floor was dead, and I was filled with sheer terror – along with the sensation that I had absolutely no control over my life. That day, I learned a valuable lesson about myself. I do not panic under pressure, in fact, I thrive. My senses slow right down and I know exactly what to do. From that day on, I made a vow to myself that I would honor the lives of all that were lost by living each day of my own life to the fullest. That's when I began to understand the power of gratitude.

For years after, I had this inner dialogue of *"why me?"* There were so many people whose lives were lost that day: mothers, fathers, grandparents, uncles, aunts, cousins, friends, people I didn't know but were loved, and yet here I still am. I had survivor's guilt because I believe that the most important job in the world is being a parent and I wasn't one. I was nineteen, and I questioned what good was I offering the world. It wasn't until ten years later that I started to talk about and process the pain, trauma and guilt from that day. It was this event that would later help me choose the business I wanted to start.

I am so grateful to say that everyone I worked with on the forty-ninth floor made it out. A big portion of that was because of the leadership and intuition of a manager who worked there, Danielle Malina-Jones. She was one of the first mentors I had in my life and working with Danielle was the beginning of a lifelong friendship with her. She is a part of my soul family. After 9/11, our office was relocated to New Hyde Park in Long Island. I kept my job working three days a week whilst going to school full time for two days. I didn't have a car back then, so Danielle would pick me up from the parking lot of Caesar's Bay in Brooklyn and we would travel to work together. It was at this point that I began to work just for a paycheck and chased the money. Yes, I sacrificed my time and suffered through work for a paycheck. The saving grace in my life is that I've always been able to have fun no matter where I am. It's a gift of mine. Even if the work sucked, I turned it into fun with music and with the people around me. Danielle and I were masters of doing that. Fun always had to be present as we were working late into the night to get the job done.

So there I was, doing whatever it took to complete projects. I was no longer doing the job of an intern, rather, I was actually working as a part-time employee but not being compensated as such. It was time to ask for a raise. I wasn't worried; money always came to me, my hours reflected how hard I worked and so did the projects I completed. It's at this moment in time that a new message of money was revealed to me. I learned that Head Office, who were located elsewhere and to whom I was just a number, had the power to say "*yes*" or "*no*" to my requested raise. I didn't get the full raise I asked for, but I stuck around even though my heart wasn't aligned with the work or the company. The money was on the whole good, and it gave me the means to get what I wanted for myself.

The final blow came after a couple of years when the corporate office decided to outsource our jobs to West Des Moines, Iowa. Apparently, it wasn't feasible to keep the Long Island office open. We went from working at the World Trade Center to experiencing 9/11 with our workplace disappearing, all the way to being out of our jobs because of it. I guess two years and a severance package justifies this action. As for me, I decided to get out of the corporate world. I clearly saw the hierarchical structure at work in the corporate environment and how divorced external corporate is to the workers. I experienced being nothing but a social security number and being in a place where a person is valued by a budget, and I wasn't a fan of that at all. Thankfully, I was able to get unemployment benefits which supported me throughout my senior year of college. I guess this is my pattern when I graduate.

Chapter 5: Woos Me Back

I graduated from Pace University with a Bachelor's degree in Business Management and a minor in Psychology. I was ready to face the world and now that school was out of the way, I could go out and make that money, full-time. I was pumped because school was never my strong suit and I discovered that I learn best experientially. Let the real learning begin, and so it did, in Dumbo, Brooklyn. Back in 2004, it wasn't so trendy to be in that neighborhood and I was there working at a startup title company. My friend Debbie was working part-time and asked if I wanted to join her. Yet again, easy money, working with my friend and getting paid cash, so it was all just perfect. This job evolved into me gaining a great deal of experience around money and the world. A title company is involved in examining and insuring title claims for real estate purposes. You need this insurance when purchasing a home. In my four years there I went from stuffing envelopes, to being the first employee (wearing all the hats), including IT, to being the Operations Manager overseeing a department of five. I assisted in growing the business from four hundred thousand closed files a month to ten million. I was constantly around financial transactions and it excited me.

I loved creating the Housing and Urban Development (HUD-1) statements for closings. Basically, it's the receipt for when you buy a house. I was the one who put all these delicious numbers on there. Crunching numbers is a turn on – yep, I'm a geek like that. I learned to process all the paperwork and money for when a house closed. We were the escrow company that held all the money. We were paying off homes worth six hundred thousand dollars to a million dollars. We would receive wires for these amounts to pay off the homes, receive letters of satisfaction, pay off debt and give the client the money that was left over from the proceeds of the sale. I adored keeping all that information tidy and organized. Seeing bank accounts with seven figures really was a thrill for me. I delighted in dispersing the money out and moving it all around. It was here that I learned to run a business from the ground up to have employees, payroll, budgets, hiring, writing up procedures and everything in between. It was here that I gained confidence and the knowledge that I was excellent at running a business. I had a knack for it.

Chapter 6: Arrogance

I was still working for the title company and my sense of determination and drive got the best of me. I was in the real estate world and in a relationship with someone who was also in that world. After two years of working in the industry, I thought it would be a great idea to buy a home with him after only knowing each other for five months. It was an investment property (there's nothing like real estate to build your money portfolio – at least that's what the investment books say). At this point I had savings, retirement and a stock account set-up. A Dividend Reinvestment Plan (DRIP) IRA like my teacher in college told me to do. I was diversifying my portfolio. I was all about making money and following the to-do list. Graduate, get a job, get a boyfriend, and then it was time for a house. Since it was an investment property, it seemed like a really good business idea.

We applied for a mortgage and were approved, which was down to the combination of my perfect credit score and my boyfriend having the money for the down payment. It was textbook. Before we knew it, we had a closing date. We bought a property in Pennsylvania so it was affordable for us, not like the housing market in New York. We figured we could rent the house out because it was in Mount Pocono and a well-known vacation spot. The cherry on top was that my best friend and her husband were buying the house next door.

Twenty-four and I am nailing my goals, I thought. Since I had the higher credit score, my name would be the only one on the mortgage note and both of our names would be on the title. Yep, even with all of my experience it still didn't register, the amount of responsibility I was taking on by having my name only on the mortgage. I was solely responsible for making the mortgage payments and if I didn't, it was *my* credit score that would be affected. I knew my boyfriend was a good, responsible man, and that he would never leave me to pay for the house on my own. For two years we had a lot of fun, enjoying the house and our "work hard, play hard" philosophy which we had perfected. Working our asses off all week, partying hard all weekend, living it up and ticking off all the boxes on my success checklist. I knew how to work my own system.

However, after a while of doing closing statements and reviewing HUD-1 statements, the numbers were no longer making sense to me. People who clearly could not afford the payments were getting approved for mortgages. How could this be? Well, the banks would come up with all these crafty loan programs of adjustable rates or the best one – the balloon payment – in order for people to afford the monthly repayment of the loan and ultimately be approved (a balloon payment is a large payment due at the end of the loan term, like a down payment but it was an end payment). So maybe a family could afford the monthly repayment, but then at the end they would still owe a chunk of the mortgage, probably needing another loan in order to pay off that chunk of money and keeping them in a vicious cycle of borrowing money. How were these borrowers ever going to be able to pay off their mortgages and own their homes?

The banks didn't care because they were selling these loans to other banks and making their money that way. This started to give me a bad vibe on the industry and the ways the banks were allowed to manipulate the numbers with all these different loan programs. It takes extreme situations, but my instincts and gut were telling me to get out and make a job change. This life was no longer sustainable or going to stay the way it was. My 9/11 experience taught me all too well to trust my instinct, and it was screaming at me to get out.

As I started to strategize and plan out my next my moves, Danielle popped into my mind. She had been asking me to work with her so that we could have fun working together again. I called her up and asked the golden question: "*How much?*" The job was going to involve a significant pay cut, so I worked my magic, crunching the numbers to reduce my personal expenses. The lease on my car would soon be up, so I planned on getting a new lease that was much lower in cost. I would cut down on the money I spent on food and fun, making my expenses work for my new salary. I took the job and gave my two weeks' notice. I knew once I was in the new job and started putting my work ethic in place that I would get the raises. Since this was a small company and not a big corporation, when I ask for a raise I was speaking directly to the decision-maker – the boss of the company – and they always viewed me as an asset. I knew my worth and I asked for it. It wasn't too long after this that the market crashed. Thank you, intuition, for leading me again.

Chapter 7: Illusions

Who knew I'd end up on Staten Island working for Priests for Life? It was here in the finance department that I learned about QuickBooks, book-keeping, account receivables, account payables and how to keep a place running when the money going out is equal to the money coming in. Working in this department shielded me from dealing with the day-to-day interaction with people. Once again, I was learning from Danielle. We had that department in tip-top shape and we knew exactly where everything was. All invoices filed away with checks stapled to the invoices, insurance policies together, employee information together, bank statements, payroll statements, and so much more. My organization skills were let out to play and I was going blissfully crazy creating checklists for every task that needed to get done: daily, weekly, monthly, quarterly and yearly. I made sure I had a list for everything so nothing slipped through the cracks.

It was my level of organization that allowed me to accomplish so much in that department as just one person. It was here that I started to develop my people skills. Since we had payables, I would have to get on the phone with vendors and negotiate. At that point I was still extremely shy and did not like to talk to people or leave voice messages. I was bullied as a kid for having a deep voice and it stuck with me. It would influence a great deal of my life in that

I would not speak up or speak at all in public. Here, I gained some confidence in using my voice and negotiating.

One day, I was sitting at my desk when I started to get pains rushing down my arm. Alarmed, I thought: *"Am I having a heart attack?"* I went to the doctor, got all the tests done and nothing was wrong with me. It was anxiety and stress from the workload I had. This is when it hit me. *"What the heck am I doing? I'm twenty-eight and working for what? To pay my bills? I'm making great money, but at what cost?"* Working a minimum of fifty hours a week and doing twelve-hour days was common – especially during an audit, at year end, during tax season or when a project came up. See the pattern? There was always an "or," and they had a strict policy on taking time off. They had blackout dates, which drove me crazy. I work my ass off – always have – and nothing is more valuable to me then my time. I started to see the trade-off. The more money I made, the more I felt I had to sell my soul or my time for it.

At twenty-eight, I couldn't imagine what my life was going to look like in five or ten years. I hit a pattern and I recognized that. I would start working at the bottom and work my way up until there was no more "up" to go. There was always going to be somebody above me telling me what I can and can't do. This just didn't work for me anymore. I was not happy – I was miserable, actually – and drinking a hell of a lot to compensate for the stress work was causing me. Yes, I was going away on vacations to escape and refill myself; however, the vacations couldn't come quick enough. Once I was back home, I simply wanted to leave again. This was not good or sustainable. I used drinking to numb that reality. Work hard, play hard.

As if thinking I was having a heart attack wasn't bad enough, there were many times that I would go to the bathroom and just cry because I was so overwhelmed with the workload. I didn't want to disappoint my friend Danielle or anyone else, so I never said anything. I was a people pleaser. Finally, I decided I was going to change the pattern. The good thing about being twenty-eight and single (yes, my boyfriend and I broke up and he kept up with the payments even though we weren't together) was my freedom. I had no one depending on me. No real responsibilities except my own.

It was here that I hit a major fork in the road. Did I choose my happiness or to be responsible? Then I thought, *Why choose – why not both?* and a third path appeared: I decided I would be responsible for my own happiness. It was this abundant mindset that supported me in starting my business. I was embracing "and" no longer "either or." Yes, I would be responsible for my own happiness and unsubscribe to societal rules. Jay-Z says it best: "*I drove by the fork in the road and went straight.*" The only reason I needed to make so much money was to cover my expenses: auto, phone, mortgage, property taxes, homeowners insurance and Homeowners Association dues. Again, I worked my magic of crunching numbers and got creative in finding ways I could cut down on my expenses.

Chapter 8: Shames Me

Let's rewind to my house in Pennsylvania, since my mortgage was the largest expense I was responsible for. Back when I bought the house, I had a "know it all" arrogance. I believed because I worked in real estate and was surrounded by real estate agents, closing agents and lawyers that I knew it all when it came to buying a home. So when my parents told me it was a bad idea, I didn't listen. They explained buying a house is a huge responsibility because of the mortgage. It went in one ear and out the other. I thought I knew better because it was a business investment, but as it turns out my parents knew a lot more than I gave them credit for. In the end they were right; clearly, I needed to learn the hard way. At age twenty-four, I didn't understand that there was a difference between intellectually "knowing" something and actually experiencing it. My parents had that experience.

Now, let's fast-forward two years to the 2008 recession. There were massive foreclosures and bankruptcies. The government had to bail out the banks and some of them were big names like JPMorgan Chase, Morgan Stanley, American Express, Goldman Sachs Group, US Bank Corp, Capital One, Bank of NY, BB&T Corp, Wells Fargo and Bank of America, to name a few: $498 billion in bailouts. There were huge companies that filed for bankruptcy: Lehman Brothers Holdings, Washington Mutual, IndyMac Bankcorp. It was bad. When this happened, the value of homes crashed and so did the value of my house in Pennsylvania. We continued to make our payments on time and for the full amount. In December of 2009, I reached out to Wells Fargo for assistance on my mortgage. The evaluation process took five months from that date. On May 6th, 2010, I received a letter from Wells Fargo stating they were unable to adjust the terms of my mortgage. The banks could receive $498 billion dollars in bailouts from the government, but for people who worked hard and paid their mortgages on time – well, you were shit out of luck! No help for you. If you were late and not making any payments on your mortgage at all, then – and only then – would they modify your loan, possibly.

I knew of many homeowners at that point who began to intentionally default on their mortgage payments, because they bought high before the crash and then the value of their house went down so much. It was humiliating. The banks could mess up and be bailed out but the people could not. Why couldn't that money be passed on to the consumer, to lower the interest rates or adjust the value of the homes? Give a one-time credit. The government did it for the banks, why not for the people? Needless to say, the banks did what they wanted with that money. If you run a search for "2008 recession," you can find many articles, news stories and documentaries on all of the corruption that took place. I was left to consider: Do I follow the rules? The rules that are broken and outdated and not aligned with looking after my wellbeing, or do I take a risk and be happy? Do I purposely default on my mortgage payments in order to have my loan modified so I can leave my job to start my own business? Crap! What should I do?

So, I decided to intentionally stop making my mortgage payments. My credit record would take a huge hit for this. I decided I was willing to let that go along with my identity of being Little Ms. Perfect. I trusted in myself and in knowing that whatever I would need my credit score for I would still find a way to get it. That's what I do; I'm resilient, relentless and resourceful. I called up my ex to let him know about my decision. When I called, he told me my timing was perfect, because he was about to have a baby and he couldn't make half of the payments anymore. In all reality, it was true that I could no longer afford my payments. Life's way of keeping me in integrity.

For a long time, that house was one of the massive "money shame" experiences in my life. Eventually, I was able to look at it as my first failed business. I learned that there is nothing like mistakes to teach me and failures to learn from. It has never been a regret that I bought the house; rather, it was a huge lesson in humility and growth. Although when I was going through this experience itself, it sure didn't feel that way!

Chapter 9: Pulls Me Back In

I did it. I left my job and opened up my business as a professional organizer: "Cut the Chaos Organizing." I incorporated it, intentionally, in September of 2011 so every time I wrote it, I would see 9/11 and remember to take a pause and appreciate the gift of my life. Then in March of 2012, I had my second near-death experience and the universe confirmed that she is definitely a comedian. It's here I started using my father's favorite mantra: "*You can't make this shit up!*"

For many months before my second near-death experience, my uncle Sante kept asking me to join this self-development workshop so I could step into my role as a leader by learning more about myself. I used every excuse not to go when he first asked me. I never had the time, and when I had the time, I told him I didn't have the money. My uncle did not let up or give up on me, and finally, he managed to persuade me. I decided to go along, and I am thankful to this day that I did because the workshop cracked my heart wide open. It gave this tin woman her heart. I'm forever grateful to Uncle Sante for being that person who held space for me to realize the power that exists in me, and to wake up to the wonder this world has to offer.

Needless to say, I was very excited to sign up for part two. It was a regular day in March, and I drove to the city in the car that I loved, my Volkswagen CC to do just that. On the way home, I was smiling from ear to ear with the combination of nerves and excitement in anticipation for what was next. I came off of the Brooklyn Bridge and got on to the Brooklyn Queens Expressway ("BQE" in short if you live in New York City). The entrance led me into the right lane of the expressway with a Budget rental truck to my left. We were driving along and then I heard this crunching sound to my left. My car was being pushed along the BQE. "*What the heck is going on????*" I remember thinking, "*This freaking truck just hit me, it really freaking hit me, it's dragging me, get off, get off!*" I had no control of my car. This damn Budget rental truck had slammed into me and was dragging me along the expressway. I didn't know it at the time, but the truck was stuck on to my car. I was petrified and didn't know what to do. Finally, the truck got free of my car and this was where the fun began.

My car started to spin out on the expressway and I have no idea how many times it did. I just remember things moving super slowly around me and my panic lessening with every spin. I took my hands off the wheel, took my foot off the pedals and I placed both feet flat on the floor. Clearly, I was not in control, nor was I going to try to be. Surrender took over and I allowed it to. The next thing I saw was the guardrail of the expressway. I'm on course for a head-on collision and there's nothing I can do about it. I was either going to live or die, and whatever the result, it had nothing to do with me. When I think back, I can't believe how much the whole accident slowed down because in all reality it was probably no more than a matter of seconds. In the moments leading up to my collision with the guardrail, a feeling of peace swept over me.

It was on this day that I learned about the many angels watching over me and present around me. Angel number one, Michael, a sanitation worker, immediately came over to my car after the collision and knocked on my window to ask if I was okay. This angel angled his truck to block off two lanes of traffic so no one would hit me while we waited for first responders. As drivers used the third lane to slowly pass, I could see the horror in their faces taking in the sight of my beautiful disaster.

Well, when I do something, I do it big!! I shutdown the entire expressway. When the fire department finally arrived, they had to use the Jaws of Life to open my car door. The fire department was incredible, I was out and immediately strapped to a board to keep my body completely still. Being surrounded by firefighters is a fantasy for some, but for me, it was a nightmare. I don't like being the center of attention. I like being invisible, a wallflower. So, I turned to my "go to" place when I'm uncomfortable: humor. I cut the tension by putting on a comedy routine for the firefighters while restrained on a board. They were all cracking up and one of them said, "*At least your spirit is still intact.*" Yes, it certainly was, and this remains a superpower of mine. I can find the silver lining in everything.

While all this was going on and unbeknownst to me, angel number two (Maureen, a complete stranger), was supporting me. She was in a car behind me when the accident took place. She pulled over to make sure I was okay and to be a witness for the police accident report. When I was finally out of the car and hanging out on the board, she came over to introduce herself and to tell me that she had documented everything for me. She said to me, "*You have some angels surrounding you and whichever side of the bed you*

slept on last night, sleep on it every night because you shouldn't have survived that accident. I thought that truck was going to push you off the expressway."
Not only did the truck not push me off the expressway, but when I began to spin out of control no cars touched me. She said, *"It's as if they were being moved out of the way so you hit no other cars."* What are the freaking odds of that? You can't make this shit up!

After that, I was put in an ambulance and taken to the hospital. It was my first ever ambulance ride and my first time going to a hospital for myself since I was born. Once all the tests were run at the hospital, I was able to get out. No internal injuries or concussions. I didn't even have a mark on my face. If you saw me while walking out of the hospital you would never had thought, *"That girl was just in a car accident."*

The next morning, I woke up sore and feeling weird. I knew something big had happened to me and that I should be resting, but I was restless and without a car. My freedom gone. There was a burn on my wrist from where the airbag popped as evidence that I was in a car accident and it wasn't just a dream. If I hadn't surrendered my arms and legs whilst in the car, those could have been two broken arms. However, a follow up doctor appointment revealed back, wrist and knee injuries. No more lifting boxes or moving anything heavy, exactly what I was doing in my new business as a professional organizer. Here I learned the tool of pivoting.

The car accident had a domino effect on so many things that impacted upon my personality and the trajectory of my life. One, the timing of it. The accident happened after I signed up to part two of the program. The message was that it's time to be the leader I knew I was and to step into my power in this program. No more playing small or acting shy. Two, receiving messages. The universe communicated with me to wake up to my power and path (especially if I'm off it) with near death experiences. Here, I started working with my aunt – the magnificent Tami Coyne – on clearing my past life experiences with the Spiritual Response Therapy (SRT) that she was certified in. I started to dip my toe into the spiritual realm and energy work, a world I was never interested in entering before this. Three, my trajectory. Since I had herniated and slipped discs at the base and top of my spine, I had to change the direction of my work. It hurt to be lifting things and bending all day long. This pain led me to doing financial organization, personally and professionally, with budgeting and bookkeeping for small businesses. Money pulled me back in, again!

Moving on to lesson number four, the universe is a comedian. I read the police report, reviewing all the details of that fateful day, and as I glanced over the information for vehicle number two I saw the name of the driver: Jackie Chen. *"Shut up! I was hit by Jackie Chen, freaking Jackie Chen!"* No, not the movie star whose name is spelled Jackie Chan with an "A." I got the message loud and clear – it was the universe's way of telling me to always remember to laugh in the face of life's problems and challenges. Don't be so serious!! Humor and laughter is everything and the secret sauce to life. Without the pivot into financial organization and bookkeeping, I would have never learned the money methodology I'm sharing with you all right here and now in this book. Talk about a silver lining right there!

Chapter 10: Onion

The next seven years in my business would take me on a journey revealing money's methodology to me, with each stage being shown to me through working with my clients and life's experiences. Who knew that walking away from corporate and the money industry would take me right back to money? Well, I guess the universe did, disguised as a professional organizer. When I went into people's homes to organize their space, I would see duplicates and triplets of things, clothes with tags still on, mail unopened, and I would always hear the client complaining that they had no money to enjoy for fun or for savings. Instantly my mind would think, *"How much money is being wasted on stuff and could be used for fun and savings instead? Money being spent on items they already have, but they don't know it, or cannot find it because of disorganization?"* This is when I realized the cost of chaos and the price being peace of mind and clarity. It made me jump for joy to know I had a solution for this cost.

I started opening people's mail and organizing their numbers. I would ask, *"Do you know what your expenses or income is? Do you know what goes in and out of your bank account?"* The answer was usually *"no."* I identified all of their numbers so they were no longer hiding behind the story of *"I don't know."* My clients then had clarity around their numbers and, once they did, amazing things began to happen. They would send me pictures of spaces in their homes that they organized on their own. Now that they knew the price of chaos, they no longer wanted it and were motivated to clear up their spaces. The connection was made in my mind and I saw that money is a linchpin. Once the money is organized, it brings clarity in all areas of a person's life. It's a domino effect. From chaos comes clarity!

Once people knew their numbers, we were able to create a structure for their money: a certain amount for living expenses, fun, and savings. They started to control where they wanted their money to go versus being a victim to it. Something very interesting – something I did not anticipate – happened as they were left in control of their money plans. As I would check in on them, it transpired that they hadn't taken action on that plan. Things may have started getting organized in their homes, but the actions to put in place for the money structure would not be followed.

I just didn't get it! They complained, I gave them a solution and yet, they were still choosing to stay in their pain instead of doing something about it. At this stage in my life. I was completely a Type A. You gave me a plan and I would destroy it, whatever it takes. It was difficult for me to understand not taking action on your goals. I would continue to go to people's homes and recreate their budgets because they were constantly being derailed from the plan. Some of the excuses I would hear were: *"Something came up, I forgot to transfer the money, I needed this new shirt, dress, shoes, TV, car, I had to go out with my friends, I had to give money to my kids,"* and the list went on and on. This was the beginning of the Focus and Foundation stages being created.

I continued doing personal financial organization and bookkeep-ing for small businesses for a few more years. After a while, it became monotonous and I had the realization that I was enabling my clients' bad habits. They wouldn't follow the plan and I would come to fix it. This pattern would repeat, over and over again. I was the drug dealer for their addiction. They had money pain and I was their fix with organization. I was living the definition of insanity. Doing the same thing and expecting a different result. I decided I was going to use my minor in psychology getting to the root of the chaos and dysfunction, not enable it. A pivot in what I was doing was about to happen.

Another thing I discovered while working with my clients was that everyone has some sort of money pain and limiting stories around money, regardless of their income. Someone with a $30,000 income had similar emotions and fears coming up around money as someone making a multiple six-figure income. The situations and circumstances were different, but the pain behind it and the feelings behind the pains were the same. Here, I had a huge "kick in the ass" moment: it occurred to me that it has nothing to do with money or the amount of it we have. It's our emotional connection to money and the experiences we had around it that determines the dysfunction of it. This blew my mind. I had never thought of it this way. Before, it was very black and white – yet now, this thought created a gray area. It was time to explore this gray area of money. The intention of this exploration was one for consistent action and sustainability on the money plans. No longer would I treat the symptom – I am here to get to the root of the problem and heal the money pain.

In 2015, that was exactly what I did. I dove deeper into emotions, habits and mindset with a number of different trainings and workshops. Each one led me to my next learning. It all began with me saying yes to Naam Yoga, a seven-month teacher training. I thought I was out of my mind because what did yoga have to do with my business?! I got honest, and I joined because I realized I needed to learn to love myself and take care of myself. This training opened up the doors and led me to the next steps I needed to take in order to have all that I dream and desire. That next step was to head to a conference for the National Association for Professional Organizers (NAPO) in Los Angeles.

At the conference, a whole new chain of events began for me when I realized I wanted to be a public speaker. It was at the opening ceremony while watching different keynote speakers on stage that I knew that this was what I wanted to do – what I would love doing. I wanted to reach the masses by talking about money and the importance of financial literacy and organization, and get the message across that we all have difficulties around money to some degree. The only problem standing in the way was figuring out how I was going to get over my fear of public speaking! No joke, it terrified me. If I spoke in public, I felt like I was going to pass out. My stomach would start churning, my palms would get all sweaty and I would get short of breath. So, the next thing I wanted to do was public speaking and yet I felt like I was going to die when I spoke in public, isn't that something. Thanks a lot, universe! And there it was, the next path on my journey had revealed itself to me: facing my fears of public speaking.

From there, I joined Red Elephant's year-long speaker training program. That took some real courage to do. Once in the speaker training program, we realized I needed to do some mindset work because I had some deep-rooted fears when it came to being seen and speaking. After that, the road led to Belanie Dishong's mindset program (another year-long training), *Live At Choice*. Little did I know that all these programs were filling my money toolbox by learning about emotions and the back end of what motivates our actions. This was all just in 2015 that the Freedom stage was being revealed to me!!

As each of these programs began to end in 2016, I decided I was no longer embarking on any other leadership and self-development training. I found myself becoming addicted to these trainings, and just wanted to take the next level so I could finally fix myself and my fear of public speaking. I realized I was on information overload and if I didn't take the time to integrate the teachings in my everyday life, it would all be for nothing. These programs were the fix, not the cure. It was time to start living the life that would make my heart sing with joy and begin to practice what I preached. This led me to traveling to two countries that same year – China and Myanmar – and those travels would end up influencing my work greatly. These experiences would in turn reveal the next stage, Flow.

Myanmar was one of these transformative experiences that came out of nowhere. When the opportunity presented itself for me to go, I knew to say yes to it because it had that magical elixir feeling of fear and excitement when it was time to book my travel tickets. It was my boyfriend at that time who was the connector for this opportunity to come my way, and I will forever be grateful for that. It was the universe's way of having fun with me, to show me a different path and the truth of money. We would travel with the World Education Foundation, whose mission is working to help global communities reshape themselves through the use of technology and education. One of their most pressing problems certain people in Myanmar had was not having electricity in their villages and also being cut off from the rest of the country when monsoon season came. The solution was teaming up with Barefoot College, an organization that trains women from villages worldwide to become solar engineers. This changed everything because when monsoon season came, they had electricity and could use cell phones to connect them to virtual doctors in cases of medical emergency.

On this trip, we were going to help conduct a WE:SOLVE lab (which is an open space, technology and design incubator focused on local youth creating local solutions) to see what this particular village still needed. I remember how the villagers were sharing what else they needed and dreamed of having for their families. We had a woman translating what they were saying. There was one particular woman who shared, that I'll never forget. Her dream was being given permission to dream again. She expressed how she didn't see the point of dreaming because they didn't have the resources or help to make them possible. Now, there were people here creating real change by teaching them the tools they need that they can sustain themselves once we were gone. She thanked us for asking her to dream. My heart broke at the thought of people around the world living without possibility. At that moment, I decided I would ask as many people as possible what their dreams are, with the hope that they would give themselves permission to dream.

Another life changing experience came from the people in the village. When we arrived there, I was struck by how they were the friendliest and happiest people I had ever met. I recall how they came over with umbrellas to shield us from the hot sun. When we got to the hut where we would conduct the WE:SOLVE lab, the villagers had a spread of all different types of food laid out for us. They treated us like queens and kings. They were so grateful for our help, and for taking the long trip to listen and support them in doing what they needed for their village. The level of gratitude they had pierced my heart. When we went exploring, we saw that each person was smiling from ear to ear, waving at us and emanating such joy. A kind of joy I had never experienced before. They showed us the school where the younger kids were learning and the children were so happy and excited. It was incredible. What I couldn't understand was how they were this happy, grateful and genuinely joyful when they lived in the conditions they existed in?

Their homes were huts made of bamboo and straw. They had no plumbing, sewer, or electrical systems besides the few solar panels the woman put up. They didn't have an abundance of food or possessions. They had what they needed and nothing more. In the school, they had a chalkboard and desks for the students – that was it. But. They. Had. Such. Joy. This confused me. How could they be so poor in the material sense and still be so rich in their soul? This is when money hit me with a four by four. *Money doesn't equal happiness.* This baffled me and I couldn't believe how wrong I had this, and how wrong we do in the United States and any country who has more than they actually need. Money doesn't equal happiness.

The people of Myanmar showed me that laughter, love, family, smiles, hugs, people and connection were what richness is. These people were only poor in the material sense. In stark contrast, their souls were rich; richer and happier than any materially wealthy person I have ever met. I returned home from this trip knowing I could no longer teach money the way I was doing it. It was time to reveal this truth about money. We put our energy, attention and focus on the material things in life and accumulate more of it and the things of real value, like those mentioned above, are all taken for granted. Was it because they had nothing that they were able to see the natural gifts all around them? I began wondering whether it was possible to experience this richness in soul without having to lose or have nothing. This began my next exploration, and this is what the Flow stage is all about.

The following year, it all came to a head and to a screeching halt when my boyfriend and I broke up and I moved back home. I was miserable. I felt like the rug was pulled out from underneath me. It was such a huge gift because I had to learn what made me happy – and not from other people or anything external. I had to get real with myself. I had to fire myself from my own business because bookkeeping was no longer making me happy. I was no longer passionate about it, and that's exactly what I told my clients when I canceled all my contracts: *"You don't want me as your bookkeeper anymore because I no longer care about the work."* My passion moved to liberating people from the obstacles of money so they can live the life of their dreams and I wanted to support them in taking that action. I decided I would do this in a playful fashion and explore the different ways I could do this for them.

This is where I began exploring playful ways, in everyday life, that brought me joys not dependent on money. I began to develop a relationship with myself where I would allow myself to experience the richness of my soul – unrelated to money. It was always a desire of mine to take a comedy improvisation course, so I took it and it was fun! That same year I got my certification in levels one and two of Reiki because I was curious about energy work. I started taking singing lessons to reclaim the joy in my voice and so that I would stop being terrified to sing in front of someone or in a car when a song I liked came on. I was on a mission of reclaiming my joy. I somehow knew that all this exploring would lead me back to what I want to do in my business and with my clients. At this point, the Fun stage began to emerge.

In 2018 it all came together when I took a program with Mama Gena's School of Womanly Arts. Here, I learned to step into my feminine power and embrace my intuition. I also learned about the traits of masculine and feminine energies, and how both are being corrupted by the patriarchy. I devoted myself to connecting with my Divine Feminine and my pussy power. I experienced the power of pleasure and living from my desires. Once I did, the money onion unraveled for me. I reached the center and I saw that each year I was uncovering an aspect of money and once I did, it showed me another layer, then another till I reached the sweet center. Now, all the layers were pulled back and it was time to test it out in the world and teach it to my clients. The *5 F's to Financial Freedom* money system was created.

Money is an onion with multiple layers, five to be exact: Focus, Foundation, Freedom, Flow and Fun. Each layer is connected and is built upon the last layer. As you peel back one layer the next one is naturally revealed to you. You don't want to skip over any layer because each one offers you a gift of reclaiming the power you gave away to money – consciously or unconsciously. Just like an onion itself, sometimes it's sweet and sometimes it can make you cry!

Chapter 11: Balance

I have two pictures that hang on the wall of my apartment from my trip to China. The first is a picture of bamboo to represent the characteristics of the masculine and the second is a red cherry blossom to represent the characteristics of the feminine. I bought the pictures at a monastery that still practices the art of calligraphy when I visited the country. When they showed me these two scrolls, my eyes instantly fell in love with the images and when I found out their meanings from the monk, my heart sang with joy. These two images are a pair: the Yin feminine and the Yang masculine, and when hung together they represent balance and harmony…exquisite! I bought these pictures to hang in my apartment as a reminder of what a healthy relationship is. This was back in 2016 when I knew nothing about balancing my own masculine and feminine traits and energy. It wouldn't be until two and half years later that I would understand the parallel of these characteristics to my life and my money system.

Mama Gena's program taught me that I have a lot more masculine traits than feminine ones. In truth, I wasn't connected to my female side; in fact, I had intentionally cut myself off from the vulnerability and weaknesses that were associated with all things feminine. I thought that if I wanted to get ahead, I had to be tough, disciplined, a goal maker, and an action taker – acting like a man, basically. I had no idea that connecting with my feminine side held the key to creativity, unconditional love and my intuition! What l learned in the years to follow and still am learning to this day is when I allow my masculine and feminine sides to dance together in unison, it creates a pure, sensational, blissful balance in my life and I get things done effectively and with fun! The same principles apply to having a balanced relationship with money. When I made this parallel, it blew my ever-loving mind and I saw that each stage in this money system has male and female traits.

A distinction I want to make on the subject of masculine and feminine traits is that they do not pertain specifically to the sex of someone determined by organs and genitalia. Every human being has masculine and feminine characteristics, regardless of sex that was assigned to them at birth, that they identity with and choose to express. Below are some of the characteristics of the masculine and the feminine traits, so you can check in to see if you lean more on one side or the other:

Some of the more masculine characteristics/traits/energies are:

strength	competitive	support
courage	protector	stability
independence	goal-oriented	clarity
leadership	rational	boundaries
assertive	linear	discipline
projective	logical thinker	capable
active	monotasking	control
giving	action taker	aggression
expansive	confidence	avoidance
outward-focused	responsibility	

gentleness	nurturing	feeling
empathy	interdependence	stillness
humility	multi-tasking	flow
receptive	patience	radiance
passive	forgiveness	surrender
contractive	unconditional	sensitivity
intuitive	love	emotional
inward	understanding	ease
compassionate	tenderness	allowing
collaborative	kindness	withholding
grateful	creativity	

Each stage in this money system has a masculine or feminine trait/energy to create balance in your relationship with money. It's not about just knowing the logical and practical side of money: the budgets, goals, sales, deadlines and spreadsheets. It's not just about knowing the intuitive and spiritual side of money: the creativity, positivity, abundance, and manifestation. Both are very important components of money. Without the masculine energy, the feminine energy never manifests – it never comes into existence. Ideas just stay ideas. Dreams just stay dreams. The masculine is all about doing and giving. The feminine is all about being and receiving. When we allow the masculine and feminine energies to play together with regard to money, we create financial harmony.

The *Five F's To Financial Freedom* is a money system will teach you to bob and weave in and out of these energies so you can have a balanced relationship with your money. You will learn the practical and intuitive side of money to be empowered around your own finances. Listed below is a guide of what to expect for each stage: the name, aim, result you'll gain, and whether it's connected to a masculine or a feminine trait. It's by completing all five stages that allow for that harmony to come through.

STAGE	AIM	RESULT	CHARACTERISTIC
Focus	Information	Clarity	Masculine
Foundation	Organization	Structure	Masculine & Feminine
Freedom	Action	New Habits	Masculine
Flow	Self-Mastery	Balance	Feminine
Fun	Celebration	Joy	Feminine

Here are some safety tips for the adventure ahead. Please keep your arms and legs in the vehicle at all times (just kidding!). In Part Two, there are worksheets and exercises for you to complete at each stage. I suggest reading the entire book first before completing the worksheets. It will be an easier experience to do this after understanding the practical side of money and feeling more empowered when approaching your finances. Throughout each stage there are sample worksheets filled out for you to get a better understanding of how this money system works and guide you along.

Move at a pace that works best for you, so you can get your money blueprint to this new paradigm. You can access the blank worksheets through my website at (**www.toniag.com/rich-resources**). Keep in mind that it's okay if it takes more than one sitting to fill a sheet in and that you can form a small money mastermind to go back to fill these sheets in with to make it fun. Now, enjoy the ride and fasten your seat belt as you enter Part Two: *The Five F's to Financial Freedom.*

Part Two:
The Five F's to
Financial Freedom

"Do what you feel in your heart to be right – for you'll
be criticized anyway. You'll be damned if you do,
and damned if you don't."

- Eleanor Roosevelt

Chapter 12: Whisperer

Throughout my seven years of running Cut the Chaos Organizing, a message from money was shown to me. I chose organization because I see everything as a puzzle, and I love putting puzzles together. Taking pieces that may seem separate and connecting them to make a whole picture. I adore turning chaos into order. My tagline was *"from chaos comes clarity."* Just as the tagline suggests, it's through the chaos that order comes. It gets messy before it gets clean – any professional organizer can tell you that! I get such joy from witnessing the clarity that organization provides and it's why I started a business doing just that. Unsurprisingly, the energy of money revealed its unique pattern to me during work with my clients. It was this message that helped create the money system I am bringing forth today. Yes, I am a money whisperer; yes, money speaks to me and yes, money travels through five stages in the form of *The Five F's*: Focus, Foundation, Freedom, Flow, and Fun!

Stage One is Focus and it's here that clarity is attained. This happens through gathering information for certain categories of your money. Do you know your numbers? Your income? Debt? Expenses? Bank accounts? Retirement accounts? Savings? Do you have savings? What were your parents' beliefs around money? What are your beliefs around money? Overwhelmed yet? Do you want to just close the book?! I understand. Trust me – those stomach-churning feelings will subside if you carry on reading. This is the very reason Focus is Stage One. It's this feeling of overwhelm that allows chaos, avoidance and giving your power away to money to reign. The beautiful aspect is that once all these questions are answered, clarity comes through, the chaos subsides and eventually goes away. You are no longer wandering in the heavy fog of turmoil. Instead, you're reclaiming your power around your numbers and choosing from a place of clarity, where all things are possible.

Here's some good news I learned from working with thousands of people. That story in your head about your money is a lot worse than what the actual numbers are. It happens EVERY time! If you think you're the only one with a money story, let me be the first to tell you that assumption is incorrect – we all have one. Now, remember the stage I told you that reigns over them all: FUN. This is the secret ingredient that makes this and all the other stages easier to complete.

> ### Tonia's Mini Money Message
> If you think you're the only one with a
> money story, let me be the first to tell you that
> assumption is incorrect – we all have one.

Money can be a painful topic. One full of shame and guilt, so bringing in fun is what allows you to stay motivated to continue moving through all the stages. Fun happens when you drop your judgment of yourself and what you're allowing the numbers to mean about you. Here's a truth bomb to support you in dropping this judgment around money….

Money is not judging you!!
Money is neutral!!
Money does not equal your worth!!

The amount of money you make has nothing to do with your worth. One has absolutely nothing to do with the other. This is a belief taken on from the world, our environment, and/or our families. Money is neutral and it is a TOOL. It shows you if something is working or not. Just like a car is a tool to get you from one point to another, so is money. If something isn't working with your money, it's not because you are stupid, dumb, or bad with it. It is simply showing you that something needs to be changed because the old way isn't working, and that's it. Please remember this as you go forward: **money is not judging you.**

From this place of clarity, you will create a vision in your mind of a life you truly want; one that makes your heart sing. The new money story you create in the Focus stage will help you to see this vision clearly. This is the early work you do in the Foundation stage before you get to the worksheets. There are two main reasons why this vision is so important. First, your dream life must be a reality in your mind's eye before it can exist in your physical reality. What you believe is what you conceive. Second, having a powerful visual of your dreams is like a great anchor that holds you steady in the storm. In this stage, the worksheets can begin to get challenging as you create the plan of your new financial system. This is why you hold the vision in your mind's eye of the life you want. It's the vision of your desired outcomes that helps you overcome the challenges.

Creating a structure for your numbers is very important. Let's say you are going on a drive, somewhere you've never been before. What's one of the first things you do? Well, if you don't want to get lost along the way, you put your global positioning system on (GPS) to show you where to go. Your money operates the same as you and without its GPS – a budget (structure) – it too will get lost. You work way too hard to have your money get lost. So, building this money blueprint is the map guiding you on the actions to take to create your dream life and reclaim your money power. This all gets done in the Foundation stage!

Amazing! You've got clarity, vision and a money plan and now it's time to take the actions to bring that plan to life. You do this in the third stage: Freedom. It's all about the actions you take to form healthy new money habits in your life. When you act from a vision, you commit to making your dreams a reality and no longer just a good idea. In the Freedom Stage, you will take the information you organized in the previous stage into your worksheets clearly listing the steps to take to form these healthy new habits. To support you in building these habits, you will start to observe your own language and realize the power of your words. Many of us believe our brains control the words we say, but very often, the words we say control our brains and influence our habits. So, we become intentional with our words and understand the value in using empowering language.

In the Freedom stage there is huge power to reclaim. You do this by listening to the words you use when you talk about money. Your words reveal the emotions you have connected to money, which is something I like to call "money pain." It can sound like this:

"I feel guilty spending my money"
"I have so much shame around my debt"
"I get so angry when I lose money"
"I feel bad asking for a raise"

You are releasing your money pain and liberating yourself from the emotional control money has over you. You control where and what you spend your money on and choose to do it with love, joy and in gratitude for your newfound freedom. From this space you enter the fourth stage, Flow.

In the Flow stage, you switch gears in learning to master another tool that directly affects your money. Here, you are discovering the greatest tool – YOU – and in doing so, you learn to create sustainable change for yourself, sustainable money habits, sustainable happiness. You learn how to manifest the income you desire and have money dates to support you working the blueprint, consistently. Did I mention it's all about sustainability here, not just a short-term fix?! Throughout, I have created exercises and tools to help you to activate your abundance and learn to listen to what is best for you by anchoring into routines.

You start to see that money is not happiness and that you create happiness for yourself. You begin see through all the illusions of money and learn who you really are, by connecting to your mind, body and soul. You learn about using breath work, meditation and sound to create a grounded state that allows you to instantly connect to abundance and happiness. You gain wisdom about how to be in control of the one thing you can control, which is the power to choose the experience you want to have around life's circumstances. You hold the power, not money. You learn to surrender, trust and have faith in who you are and allow yourself to receive from the universe.

Tonia's Mini Money Message
Money is not happiness.
You create happiness for yourself.

The fifth stage is Fun, and remember, this stage permeates through them all. Fun is not an experience just saved for the end when you complete something. Fun is an experience you create whenever you want and throughout the journey. This is how you thrive instead of just survive. Money can be playful and is playful. Its true purpose is to be an expression of love and a way for you to say thank you for the things you have in your life. This may sound a bit "wooey." It's okay if it does sound that way – when I first learned it, I thought so too. I want you to understand that this concept doesn't develop overnight. It starts to come through gradually when you allow yourself to play with life and follow your curiosity. This allows for new perspectives and discoveries to emerge. You learn to celebrate each step you take, each victory and mistake.

Don't worry – at the end of each category, I'll have celebration moments and *Fun Tips* for us to start flexing this muscle. What also makes things fun is doing things in community and no longer doing it alone. It's improvising with life and with others. In the Fun stage, you learn to do all of these things. This is what allows a new playful perspective to come through about money and experiencing it as an expression of love and gratitude.

Every day I commit to myself that I will live life in this truth and the grass is so much greener on this side. So, be easy with yourself if it feels awkward at first. It *is* awkward, because this isn't what we are taught about money. This discomfort and awkwardness can also be a feeling that deep down inside, you've always known this to be the truth of money too! Whatever it is, and wherever you are, it is perfect and is happening in its own divine timing for you. As we roll into the five stages, remember you can do this at your own pace. Remember the names for these Five Stages are not by accident. The journey is to Focus on your story and your numbers, so you have a healthy Foundation for your new money system to be built on with a clear vision and plan. You step into your Freedom with each action you take and money pain you reclaim, so you can be in Flow with life and have Fun with your money. It is now time to begin your money empowerment journey. First stop, Focus!

Chapter 13:
Stage One - Focus

The first stage is all about getting clarity on your finances. We do this through the process of identification because once we know what all our numbers are, we are no longer giving our power away to money by saying, "*I don't know.*" At this stage, the conversations around money disorganization sound like this: "*I don't know what my numbers are. I don't know where my money goes. I don't know what accounts I have. I don't know how much I spend every month. I don't know how much debt I have. I don't know how to save.*" All these different forms of "*I don't know.*" The very first thing we want to do is change this limiting story of "*I don't know*" to "*I know what all my numbers are!*"

It sounds simple enough, but – we tend to not do anything about it because there's a limiting story running in the background keeping us safe from the emotions surrounding money: shame and guilt, to just name two. Here's a fun fact: everyone has experienced money shame at one point or another, and the feeling of money shame does not discriminate by the amount of money we have. When I worked with clients, whether their income was large or small, the stories around money were similar. That's why during this stage, we change our money story. Your money story is what you believe to be true about money, for you. It's this narrative that's running the show in your life and that's why it is the first thing we change (focus on). The second thing we embrace in this stage is responsibility.

This responsibility begins with identifying the six main categories of money that we use on a day-to-day basis: mindset, accounts, debt, expenses, income, and savings. We activate using money as a tool to show us if something is working or not. Our numbers are here to tell us a story and it wants to show us what to do next. The focus is not about the emotions, but about gathering information so we know what to do next! This applies to all six categories in this stage. At times, this can be painful. Money pain is a real thing, but instead of focusing on it, we are choosing to focus on the clarity and peace of mind we're gaining.

You are choosing to create clarity from chaos. You are saying "bye-bye" to mind and money disorganization. If you are still intimidated, that's okay and it's the reason why I am here to support and guide you along the way because chaos is my playground. I love chaos and it's one of my favorite places to play in. I know that chaos is the call for change, and change is exhilarating. In his book *The Big Leap*, Gay Hendricks describes something called your "genius zone" which is your unique power area. What I learned is that chaos is one of my genius zones. So, allow me to play in your chaos, and buckle your seat belt because you are about to commence on a liberating and fun journey with money. I want you to practice from the very first stage being non-judgmental around your finances: leave the judgment at the door.

Mindset Money History

The first stop on this journey is looking at our money history. We identify the limiting money story running in the background of our minds by answering a series of questions about our external environment while we were growing up. As children, we absorb so much, and we have beliefs that exist from our parents, friends, school, church and whatever else we're around. These thoughts are running unconsciously in our minds, creating the experiences we have in our lives. We want to stop this now and we can! The intention is to become aware of our money story and rewrite it. By becoming aware of our unconscious thoughts, we can rewrite the script into one that we choose, not inherit. This is what identifying our money history is all about. We will use the **Money History Worksheet** further down below to rewrite our negative money stories into healthy ones.

You are reframing your money story to reclaim your money power. This exercise below will help you understand why it is so important for you to reframe in order to reclaim. It's easier for you to experience what I mean than to explain it. Please read the below narrative and as you do, take notice of how you feel, your body's reaction, and your facial expression.

> I suck at managing my finances.
> I am never going to get out of debt.
> I am not responsible with my money.
> I don't know how to save.
> I don't know where my money goes.
> I always spend my savings.
> I do not have a plan for my money.
> I am scared to charge more for my services.

I am ashamed of my debt.
Money is out of my control.
Living off a budget is limiting.
If I have too much money, the government will take it away.
Money is not spiritual.
I can't do what I love and make money.
Other people can be wealthy, but I can't.
Meaningful work doesn't get you paid.
Rich people are superficial, wasteful, and exploitative.

How did you feel reading those statements? Was your body in an open or closed position? Did it feel comfortable or uncomfortable reading this? Were you smiling or frowning? If you like, you can take a moment to journal in the back of the book on these questions.

Next, please read the below narrative and as you do, again take notice of how you feel, your body's reaction, and your facial expression.

I am great at managing my finances.
I am debt-free.
I am responsible with my money.
I know how to save and I do it magnificently.
I know where all my money goes.
It is safe to save money.
I have a plan for my money.
I charge more easily and effortlessly.
I am grateful for my debt.
I am empowered around money.
Living off a budget is freeing.
I give my money to the government as an expression of my
gratitude for the abundance I receive.

Doing what I love brings me great money.

I am wealthy.

I get paid for meaningful work.

Money creates connection, abundance, kindness and dignity.

I serve the world when I make money.

Again – how did reading these statements make you feel? Is your body in an open or closed position? Did it feel comfortable or uncomfortable to read those words? Were you smiling or frowning? Pause and take real notice. If you are unsure, read the statements again, slower this time. Afterwards, you can once more take a moment to journal in the back of the book on these questions, if you would like to.

One narrative has you living in scarcity and the other one in possibility. Imagine living every day from the first narrative. Those thoughts repeating in your mind a hundred times a day. What do you really think you are creating around money from this narrative? If it were a relationship, what type of relationship would you have with money? A poor one or a healthy one? I would conclude that it would be a poor one. The crazy reality is, this is where you are creating from right NOW!! But don't panic, you are not broken or screwed. Be relieved. You just figured out what's not working and the cause of the dysfunction. Take a deep breath and release it. I'll say it again. You just figured out what's not working and the cause of the dysfunction. Celebrate the heck out of that!!! It's important for you to know the root of where your actions take place, and the incredible Joe Dispenza breaks down why perfectly: *"Clear intention (focus & foundation stage) + elevated emotion (freedom stage) = manifestation (flow stage)."* As long as you say you can't, you won't be able to. The first order of business in your money journey is to change the way you think about money, creating a clear intention. This is money empowerment in action.

Below you will be working on a Money History Worksheet, but before we begin, I want to dive deeper into four of the questions from this worksheet.

#8. List three things you would have if money was not an obstacle.

This is teaching you to dream without money's permission and to allow your desires to come forth without restriction. It allows you to flex your imagination and dream muscles. In my experience, this is something we as people do not take the time often enough to do or even at all, and that is detrimental to the concept of money being fun! We will go further into this in the next stage, Foundation. For now, we are baby stepping it and going with just three things we desire.

#9. If you suddenly had to evacuate your home, which three things would you grab? *(Your family counts as one answer, you do not have to list out each family member.)*

This question prompts you to center into what you really value. Unfortunately, it takes extreme situations, like a fire, a flood or pandemic to realize what's really important to us. It's when I did my volunteer work for hurricane Sandy that I learned this. People lost all they had but were grateful to have their families safe. Everything else can be replaced, our loved ones cannot. I don't want you to have to be in an extreme situation to put into perspective what really matters for you.

#10. What did you notice about your answers in question 8 versus question 9?

This question asks you to compare your answers in numbers 8 and 9. The purpose is to see if the money you are spending is in alignment with what you value. The answers in number 9 show you what you value. The answers in number 8 are what you believe will make you happy. Are the things you listed in question number 8 adding value to your life or are just things you want for status and approval?

#11. List five negative conversations you have around your money. *If you have more than five, please list them, but we want at least five as a minimum.*

This is where most people get stumped. Our minds are tricky little things, and sometimes when we are put on the spot, they can conveniently go blank, and it's happened to me, many times. In case you find yourself struggling to write down some answers when you get to this question, here are some tricks to entice them out. Think about the amount of money you currently make. Are you happy with that amount? Think about the amount of money you want to make and now listen to the thoughts in your mind. Maybe you hear, *"You'll never make that amount without killing yourself first,"* or some other version.

Whatever it is, write it down. Another scenario, imagine yourself paying bills: What thoughts arise? Write down those thoughts. When you ask for a raise, what thoughts come through? Also, see what you wrote for question number one: *What challenges do you face in getting financially organized?* Usually, there are statements here that reflect limitations around money. They can sound like, *"I suck at finances,*" or "*I have no savings.*" These are the negative statements to write down for question number 11.

#12. Rewrite each of these into a healthy money conversation.

Now, for the fun part. I want you to reframe to reclaim! This is a tool I want you to learn and put into practice in your everyday life. Repeat after me: "*Reframe to reclaim!*" What you do is rewrite the negative statement into a positive one. When first trying this, you can get hung up on it being perfect – many of my clients do and so have I – but don't worry, I am here to support you. If you have the statement, "*I suck at finances,*" you are going to replace the word that is disempowering (suck) and replace it with a word that is empowering. Simply, what is the opposite of "suck"? How about good? So, our new statement is "*I'm good with finances.*" Write this statement down by question number 12.

> **Tonia's Mini Money Message**
> Reframe to Reclaim!

Here's another example: "*I have no savings.*" What's the disempowering word here? It's "no," and what word replacing "no" will make you feel empowered? How about "plenty": "*I have plenty of savings,*" or just remove the "no" and it becomes "*I have savings.*" See, you're getting the hang of it now. If you need support in finding the opposite word, go to Google, type in your disempowering word along with the word "antonym." Choose the word that best fits your statement. Make sure the statement resonates with you and feels good when you say it. The power comes from the words resonating with you.

Below is the **Money History Worksheet**, which will take ten to fifteen minutes when you fill it out. Once you have completed these questions, the answers will reveal the money story running your life, and create real change in that moment because it is now in your awareness. So, when you do it give yourself permission to speak your truth because at that very moment, you can take your power back around money. Are you going to take it back? I say, "*Hell yes!*"

*To download a blank version of the money history worksheet, go to **www.toniag.com/rich-resources**

"My favorite things in life don't cost any money.
It's really clear that the most precious resource
we all have is TIME."

– Steve Jobs

MONEY HISTORY WORKSHEET

1. What challenges do you face in getting financially organized?

- *I don't know where to start to get my money in order.*
- *I can't save.*

2. List three ways you would like to improve your money management.

- *I have a budget for my money.*
- *I am saving money.*

3. Growing up, what were your father/father figure's money beliefs and relationship with money?

Making a lot of money will change you. More money, more problems.

4. Growing up, what were your mother/mother figure's money beliefs and relationship with money?

Saved and budgeted money. Counted every dollar.

5. Growing up, what were the money beliefs of your friends and community you grew up in? What was their relationship with money?

You work hard and you can make money.

6. Do you see any connection between your parents' money beliefs & your own?

Yes, I micro-manage my money and believe more money creates more problems.

7. Do you see any connection between your friends and community's money beliefs & your own?

Stuck in the rat race of doing more to make more.

8. List three things you would have if money was not an obstacle.

- *House in the country.*
- *Traveling.*

9. If you suddenly had to evacuate your home, which three things would you grab?

- *My loved ones.*
- *My pets.*

10. What did you notice about your answers in question 8 versus question 9?

In Question 8 I focused on security and in question 9 I focused on relationships.

11. List five negative conversations you have around your money. If you have more than five, please list them, but we want at least five as a minimum.

- *Living off a budget is limiting and hard.*
- *I don't know where my money goes.*

12. Rewrite each of these into a healthy money conversation.

- *Living off of a budget is freeing and easy.*
- *I know where my money goes.*

Great job in answering those questions. What was revealed to you when you did? Did you see a similarity between what your father (or father figure) said about money and the things you say to yourself or others about money? Did you see a difference in what your mother (or mother figure) said about money and the things you say to yourself about money? Do some things sound the same as the language of your friends, school or even church growing up? There is no right or wrong here, just truth and raw honesty.

Release the judgment. Invite the money story that's running unconsciously in your mind, repeating multiple times a day, day in and day out, to reveal itself to you. This way, it is now in the light of your awareness.

You now have a new money story, one that is both positive and empowering. Go and have some fun writing the new money story out. Use stickers, colored pens or pencils, whatever will evoke the feeling of joy. It can be on a piece of paper, index card, sticky note, whatever feels good for you, and place it somewhere you will see it every single day. Daily, read these statements aloud. At first it may feel unnatural to read them or vocalize them – that is precisely why we're doing this. We want the new money story to feel as natural as brushing our teeth in the morning. It's through repetition that we achieve this. Joe Dispenza says it best: *"A habit is a redundant set of automatic, unconscious thoughts, behaviors and emotions that's acquired through repetition."*

You are not faking it until you make it. The effect of that expression is that it has you feeling like an imposter in your own body, and it allows your external circumstances to validate when you "make it." Instead, you are repeating it until you believe it! You are choosing to be intentional with your actions and are using the power of your mind to create your reality, to control the things you can control. Therefore, repeat it until you believe it! This is our new mantra.

> **Tonia's Mini Money Message**
> Repeat it until you believe it!

Soon, these statements will no longer be stories – rather, they will be the reality you live in. You are choosing the things in your internal world that you want to manifest in your physical outer reality. To enhance this, you can use the tool of visualization by closing your eyes and imagining yourself doing the things in your new money story. You do not have to imagine all of them at once. You can choose one statement a week to visualize on. It's time to live the empowering money story.

Now, take a moment and celebrate yourself for reading through this section and the work you just did. You are magnificent. Well done! Huge work has been done and this is just the beginning. A great way to celebrate is with some fun and play! As you write your new money story, embody the spirit of a child and use color pencils, pens, colored paper, or even stickers. Whatever feels good and reflects fun for you. The goal is to infuse it with the energy of JOY and to get excited just looking at your new story because it's so vibrant.

> **FUN TIP:** I invite you to give yourself permission to be silly in writing out your new money story and vocalizing it with attitude! Heck, go crazy and visualize the statement that lights you up the most.

Accounts Information

The second stop on this money journey is account information. Here, you identify all the accounts you have: checking, savings, retirement, investments, certificate of deposit (cd's) and whatever else that's a holding mechanism for your money. The focus is not supposed to be the amount of money in these accounts, but about gathering the information for each and every one. No longer will you say, "*What accounts do I have?*" or "*Which company is my retirement savings with?*" Nor will you say, "*My account information is all over the place*" or "*How much is in my savings, checking, etc.?*" You are removing the narrative of "*I don't know*" and creating the narrative of "*I know*" by putting all your information in one place to live in, which is where the **Accounts Information Worksheet** below comes in.

"The real purpose of money is to express appreciation
for the magnificence of yourself as the Creator of
everything you experience and the magnificence of
all your creations as you create & experience them."

– Robert Scheinfeld

ACCOUNTS INFORMATION WORKSHEET

What to Do: Gather the following information for all your accounts and fill in the fields below for your bank accounts, retirement accounts, investment accounts.

Then, enter the purpose of each account. Here are suggestions: bill pay, debit card, fun account, direct deposit, emergency savings, long term savings, retirement, taxes.

Some of your accounts might currently have more than one purpose. This is something we will address later when we sharpen the focus of your accounts.

Name	Acct #	Type	APY %	Min. Balance	Fee	Balance
Bank XYZ	0567	Checking	0%	$100	$15	$500

Purpose of Account: Pays bills, debit card, direct deposit

Name	Acct #	Type	APY %	Min. Balance	Fee	Balance
Bank XYZ	0310	Savings	.50%	$0	$0	$1300

Purpose of Account: Savings

*To download a blank version of the accounts information worksheet, go to **www.toniag.com/rich-resources**

All you do for this worksheet is fill in the blanks to the best of your ability. The first piece of information to identify is the *Name* field, write down the name of the institution or bank holding your money, e.g. "TD Bank" or "Chase." For the *Account #*, type in the last four digits of that bank account, this way it makes it super clear to know which account you're using if you bank at the same place. For *Type*, fill in what type of account it is: checking, savings, retirement, investments, or CD. Your *APY* (annual percentage yield) is the rate of return the bank is paying you for the money you keep with them. It's always good to know what your money is earning for you.

After that the next field is *Minimum Balance*. Here, I want you to fill in the amount of money you are required to keep in that account in order to not get charged a fee. To find this information, type into a search engine the name of your bank, the type of account you have and "minimum balance requirement" and this information should come up (or there will be a link to where you can find this information). After you find out the minimum balance requirement, find out the fee they charge you once you go below that balance. Put that amount in the next field, *Fee*. This way you know the fees your bank is charging you. I had a client of mine save an extra $105 a month in fees because they knew the balance to keep and then did. Yes, there are banks that charge no fees and we will get into that in the Foundation stage.

Next we have *Balance*. Here, fill in the amount of money you currently have in that specific account. The point of getting this information is so you can transform from saying "*I don't know*" to "*I know!*" Our money power lives in the clarity of knowing. Imagine how great it will be when you know all your financial information. If you're worried about finding this information, there are two simple options. If you have access to your accounts online, log into your accounts and access these details. If you do not have online access, when the next statement comes in, grab that statement, open the envelope and fill in this sheet. No biggie. One more field to go and you're done with this worksheet.

Lastly is *Purpose of Account*. Here, you write the purpose of what this particular account is. What do I mean by this? Is your checking account the main account where you pay your bills out of? If so, this would be your "Bill Pay Checking." Is your debit card associated with another checking account? If so, this account would be your "Debit Card Account." If your debit card is attached to the account you pay bills out of, then it would be your "Bill Pay and Debit Card Account." Is there an account where you receive your paychecks, an account for fun, emergency savings, retirement, etc.? (Don't worry if this all seems too much, in Stage Two I will go over in detail the importance and purpose of each account). The name of the game is to identify all the accounts you have money in so you are no longer living in financial fog and moving into financial clarity. We identify to clarify.

Tonia's Mini Money Message
We identify to clarify.

Time to celebrate yourself for reading through and completing the second category. To add some life into this mechanical activity of gathering our numbers, let's bring in some fun, do a little wiggle or dance when you fill in the balance for your accounts.

FUN TIP: A song I love to listen to when getting into money doing mode is Fifty Cent, "I Get Money." Pick a song about money that excites you. When things get too mechanical, play your money song to break it up.

Tonia's Mini Money Life Lessons

I'm Tired

I'm tired. I'm tired of settling to life's circumstances, to my limiting stories, to my emotions. I'm tired of reacting and allowing that to determine my outcome. I'm tired of giving my power away – no, I'm tired of being afraid of my power. I'm tired of fearing getting everything I ever wanted. I'm tired of being afraid of the unknown and not trusting myself. I'm tired of settling for life's breadcrumbs – I'm ready for the pie.

Debt Information

Welcome to the third stop: debt. Here is a place where many feelings of shame and guilt can dwell, robbing you of your peace around money. In this stage, you focus on gathering the numbers without adding any stories to it. You are dropping the judgment around your debt. The chatter can sound like this: *"I am so ashamed of my debt." "I can't believe I have this much in debt." "How did I get in debt?" "I am so bad with money."* These are just a few I have heard and experienced myself. I want you to know these stories are not true. They live by the judgment you attach to it. Let's allow your debts to just be numbers and information showing you that something is or is not working, nothing else.

A big reason we are fearful around money is because we choose to avoid instead of confronting what our numbers really are. We choose to stay stuck in "I don't know" and what we are missing out on by avoiding our debt is the freedom to be free of it! You can't pay something off if you don't know what your balances are to pay off. Here's some light to get you through the dark debt tunnel. Countless times that I've done this with my clients, the number they had in their head for the total debt they owed was always more than what the number really was. That's why clarity is so important, it busts the myth you are creating in your head.

Tonia's Mini Money Message
That's why clarity is so important, it busts
the myth you are creating in your head.

For some of us, we know the numbers and still don't know what to do with our debt. Allow me to tell you this is normal because strategies to pay off debt and financial literacy are not taught in schools when they absolutely should be! To put things in perspective, as of November 2020, the United States is in $27 trillion worth of debt. From the top down, there is a crisis in debt, so if you have some judgment coming up, drop it, please. We are doing the best we can and by reading this book, we are changing your relationship with money. Let's continue learning all we can and empower ourselves around the topic of money even more.

If you have no debt, go you, but I suggest continuing to read because you never know what you might pick up.

Below you will use the **Debt Information Worksheet** to put your debt numbers into.

You are identifying the credit cards, credit lines, student loans, mortgages, car loans and anything else you owe money on. The information to enter is the name of the creditor, the APR (annual percentage rate), due date, balance, minimum payment amount, interest amount, and the current payment method (identifying which bank account you pay that specific debt out of). Remember, drop the judgment and focus on gathering the numbers. The numbers are just here to guide you, so go ahead and let them.

Joy Tips:
Leave your judgment at the door. You are doing great!
Let's practice using money as a tool to say thank you.
Think of the above items this debt paid for and say
thank you for those things and experiences.

DEBT INFORMATION WORKSHEET

What to do: Gather information from your debt: credit cards, credit lines, student loans, mortgage, etc. and fill it in the worksheet below.

Creditor	APR %	Due Date	Balance	Minimum Payment	Interest Amount	Current Payment Method
Visa	19.99%	16th	$3400	$90	$57	Acct 0567
Discover	14.99%	20th	$1850	$41	$23	Acct 0567
Macy's	25.99%	13th	$5000	$158	$108	Acct 0567
Chase	14.99%	5th	$6500	$146	$81	Acct 0567
TOTAL			**$16750**	**$435**	**$269**	

*To download a blank version of the debt information worksheet, go to **www.toniag.com/rich-resources**

———————————

"Money is a great translator of intention to reality, vision to fulfillment."

- Lynne Twist

———————————

The first item on this worksheet is *creditor*. Here, you write the name of the credit card company, person or loan establishment you are paying money back to. Next is the *APR*. Credit card companies are notoriously tricky with this information, so it will not be somewhere obvious like page one of your statement or the homepage when you log in online. Usually, it's on the fine print page of your statement – either page two or three after the list of your transactions. Your annual percentage rate or APR is the amount of interest the creditor is charging you for the money it has lent to you. If you do not pay the balance off in full every month, you get charged one twelfth of that percentage rate. On your credit card statement, there is a line item that tells you this information and lists the monthly amount charged and the total amount of interest charged for the year. This information is very useful to know.

If you are curious to know more about how they came up with these figures, here is an example to support you. You go to your statement and you see your annual percentage rate is 24%, which is on the high side. Every month, if you don't pay off your balance in full, they charge you 2% on the full balance of the account. If your balance on one of your debts is $5,000 you're being charged $100 a month in interest alone. Below is a breakdown to show you how to figure out what your monthly APR is and the monthly interest amount for your debt.

Monthly Percentage Rate for APR Formula:

24% (APR) divided by 12 (number of months in a year) = 2% (monthly APR)

Monthly Interest Amount Formula:

$5,000 (balance amount) x

2% (monthly interest rate) =

$100 (monthly interest)

It can get a little thick in this stage, possibly creating information overload. If that happens, stop and take a deep breath in and then out. Remember, clarity paves the way for financial freedom – so let's keep identifying and filling in the information for the worksheets.

The next item to identify is *Due Date*. If you don't make your payment on time, you will get charged a late fee, which is why it is super useful to know this information. An average late fee is $36 so they can add up and become costly. Two late payments a month and that's $72 down the drain. No thank you to that!

After this is *Balance*, and here we identify the total amount of money you owe to the creditor. After that is *Minimum Payment*, and this is the lowest amount you are responsible to pay on the debt to avoid getting charged a late fee. Continuing to make these payments on time is what keeps us in good standing with the credit bureau and one factor that influences our credit score. Next is *Interest*, and I explained above where to find this information on your statement. Last is *Current Payment Method*, which is the bank account you pay this bill out of. Also, on the bank account line, identify if you make the payment manually every month or if it is automatically withdrawn from your account.

Celebration moment! We are now done with identifying all the information we need for our debt! Go us, we are no longer giving our power away to *"I don't know!"* Keep going, you are doing amazing! The point is to have the numbers in your awareness so you can begin making the changes to get you debt-free. Yes, it IS possible and in Stage Two, Foundation, you will learn the strategy to pay down your debt. Let's bring in some fun to celebrate by going outside and doing something you enjoy.

FUN TIP: Something I enjoy doing as fun is going out and playing on swings! What free fun will you choose?

Expense Information

Welcome to your expenses category. Here, the intention is to get clear on what you spend your money on. The focus is not to judge the amount being spent, but to bring awareness to where you are spending your money – therefore, you can make a conscious decision on how you want to spend it. Before we begin identifying your expenses, we will bring in some gratitude to counter that judgment. This way you can practice using money as a tool to say thank you! The definition of money according to Merriam-Webster is: "*Something generally accepted as a medium of exchange, a measure of value, or a means of payment.*"

Money was created because people needed a way to measure the amount to exchange for goods and services. Money is just one form of currency and a way to say thank you for the goods and services you give and receive. Other currencies are people's time, bartering for services, and love. So remember, money is just one form of currency and gratitude is the golden ticket to abundance and peace of mind.

Tonia's Mini Money Message
Gratitude is the golden ticket
to abundance and peace of mind.

A great way to practice treating money as a way to say thank you in your everyday life is to acknowledge that every time money leaves your hand, you are saying thank you for the service or goods the other person provided to you or you provided them. How cool is that?! When you go and buy coffee from the store, recognize, when you hand the attendant your money, you are saying, *"Thank you"* for this coffee. That's the exchange. The giving to receive. When you are paying your bills – rent, for example – a beautiful ritual to practice is saying, *"Thank you for this roof over my head,"* as you write the check or send out that payment to your landlord, or to the bank for your mortgage. Below is an explanation of the power of gratitude written by Melody Beattie in her book, *The Language of Letting Go*, where she explains so eloquently the power of gratitude.

Gratitude

Say thank you, until we mean it.

Thank God, life, and the Universe for everyone and everything sent your way.

Gratitude unlocks the fullness of life. It turns what we have into enough, and more. It turns denial into acceptance, chaos to order, confusion to clarity. It can turn a meal into a feast, a into gifts, failures into successes, the unexpected into perfect timing, and mistakes into important events. It can turn an existence into a real life, and disconnected situations into important and beneficial lessons. Gratitude makes sense of our past, brings peace for today, and creates a vision for tomorrow.

Gratitude makes things right.

Gratitude turns negative energy into positive energy. There is no situation or circumstance so small or large that it is not susceptible to gratitude's power. We can start with who we are and what we have today, apply gratitude, then let it work its magic. Say thank you, until you mean it. If you say it long enough, you will believe it.

Every time money leaves our hands, we can have this powerful experience. Using gratitude is a tool that allows us to transform our relationship with money. Imagine what a different experience you will have with money and paying your bills when you come through the lens of gratitude. Money is so incredible! We begin to see that a different way is possible with our money. That's what the Focus stage is all about and why identifying your numbers is the first step in this process. This is what the power of clarity brings to our lives. We again shift the narrative of *"I don't know where my money goes"* to *"I know exactly where my money goes!"* You are building the road map for your money because without a map, your money will get lost.

Below is a sample of the **Expense Information Worksheet** for you to put all your expense information in, this way you can start drawing your expenses map. The columns are broken down into *Expenses, Amount, Due Date* and *Current Payment Method.*

EXPENSE INFORMATION WORKSHEET

What to do: Gather the expense information from your bill and bank statements and fill it in the worksheet. The expenses are broken into groups of **Needs, Wants**, and **Fun**.

NEEDS			

EXPENSES	AMOUNT	DUE DATE	CURRENT PAYMENT METHOD
Grocery	$400	-	Debit card - Acct 0567
Mortgage/Rent	$1800	1st	Bank XYZ - Acct 0567
Car Insurance	$100	23rd	Bank XYZ - Acct 0567
Car Payment	$250	25th	Bank XYZ - Acct 0567
Gas (Car)	$60	-	Debit card - Acct 0567
Tolls / EZ Pass	$40	-	Discover Credit Card
Electric	$100	20th	Bank XYZ - Acct 0567
Gas	$100	19th	Bank XYZ - Acct 0567
Internet	$80	21st	Visa Credit Card
NEEDS Total	**$2930**		

WANTS

EXPENSES	AMOUNT	DUE DATE	CURRENT PAYMENT METHOD
Cable TV	$120	30th	Bank XYZ - Acct 0567
Cell Phone	$100	5th	Bank XYZ - Acct 0567
Donations	$50	-	Bank XYZ - Acct 0567
All Debt Payments	$435	-	Bank XYZ - Acct 0567
Toiletries	$120	-	Debit card - Acct 0567
WANTS Total	**$825**		

FUN

EXPENSES	AMOUNT	DUE DATE	CURRENT PAYMENT METHOD
Classes/Workshops	$75	-	Debit card - Acct 0567
Clothing	$100	-	Macy's Credit Card
Entertainment	$100	-	Discover Credit Card
Gifts	$50	-	Debit card - Acct 0567
Gym Membership	$75	16th	Discover Credit Card
Hair	$60	-	Discover Credit Card
Nails	$100	-	Debit card - Acct 0567
Restaurant/Takeout	$500	-	Visa Credit Card
Subscriptions	$50	-	Discover Credit Card
FUN Total	**$1110**		

*To download a blank version of the expense information worksheet, go to **www.toniag.com/rich-resources**

"Our prosperity as a nation depends upon the personal financial prosperity of each of us as individuals."

– George S. Clason

In the first column, you have a list of items that are considered expenses. They are further broken down into groups: *Needs*, *Wants* and *Fun*. The breakdown of the groups is super important because a lot of us today think we *need* a lot more than we do. We mistake "want" or "fun" with "need." The Covid-19 pandemic showed us exactly what our real needs are. All our bodies truly need to live are air, food, water, shelter, and our loved ones.

In the group *Needs*, the expenses are food/groceries, health insurance, home/renters' insurance, mortgage or rent, transportation and utilities. It's the things we truly cannot live without. After that comes our *Want* items. These are the items we mistake as needs, but we can live without them. What they provide is comfort. Under this category we have cable television, cell phone, childcare, co-pay/deductibles, donations, laundry or dry cleaning, minimum amount for debt payments (put the "total amount of minimum payments" number from your debt worksheet here), medical/prescriptions, savings, toiletries, and taxes. I know some of you will be looking at these thinking I'm a crazy lady. Some people really do need their prescriptions. Yes, but sometimes there are other options available that are less costly. The point of putting it under this group is that it's negotiable. We are at choice in the *Want* category, even if the choice makes us uncomfortable.

After *Wants* comes *Fun*. This is everything you spend your money on for enjoyment. Some of the items that fall in this category are classes/workshops, clothing, entertainment, gifts, gym, hair, life insurance, nails, personal spending/cash, restaurant/takeout, subscriptions, vacations and other enjoyable items because everybody has different things they like to do. We put them under *Fun* to acknowledge that the item we are spending the money on is fun! Let's not rob ourselves of the experience of joy.

The next column to identify is *Amount*. Here, we enter the specific amount of that expense. Expenses are either fixed or can vary in the amount. A fixed expense is a bill that's amount does not change from month to month. Examples of expenses that tend to be fixed are rent, phone, internet and cable, to name a few. A variable expense is a bill where the amount changes each month. Examples of expenses that tend to be variable are electric, gas, gas for your car, and groceries. An easy way to remember is fixed expenses stay fixed in amount and variable expenses will vary in amount – it's in the root of the word.

I recognize you might reach a predicament when identifying your variable expenses. What amount do you put in, considering the amount of the expense varies from month to month? I have a solution for that. For all your variable expenses, we will take a three-month average. Doing this gives you an accurate read for the monthly fluctuations and it's a good length of time because it represents a quarter of a year. As an example, let's take your electric bill. We will take the amount of the previous three months, add them up and then divide that number by three. Follow the formula below:

$90 (month 1 amount) + $130 (month 2 amount) + $80 (month 3 amount) = $300 (total of 3 months)

$300 (total of 3 months) divided by 3 (number of months) = $100 (monthly average for that expense)

Using this example, $100 is the figure that goes into the worksheet under *Amount* for your electric. You will do this for all the expenses that vary from month to month like gas, groceries, restaurants, clothes, etc. The great thing about being in a world ruled by plastic and electronic information is that you can easily find this information on your debit card, bank account statement or credit card statement – it's easily accessible. Also, look out for any expenses that are not covered on the list above when going through your statements. The expenses listed are the most common, but you are unique in your spending. So, when you find an expense not covered, please add it to the expense information sheet under *Other*.

The next column, *Due Date*, is for the date the expense is due every month. Some expenses will be fixed and some will vary in the date they are due. Fill in the information for those expenses with fixed due dates. They are typically your utilities, rent, insurances, credit cards and car payment. You can find this information on the bill for that expense or if it is an automatic withdrawal, go to your bank statement and look at the date it is taken out every month. The due dates that vary you will leave blank. The final column is the *Current Payment Method*. Here, you put the name of the account the expense gets paid out of (cash, credit card, bank account) and if it gets withdrawn automatically or paid manually.

I know this seems like a lot – it is, but you are doing great!! Many people find that the Focus Stage is the hardest one and that it gets easier as they progress through each stage. The benefit of knowing your numbers far outweighs the pain you are feeling right now. You are reclaiming your power here. Through clarity comes freedom. Please keep repeating that when you feel like stopping. Through clarity comes freedom. Through identification comes clarity, hence why you keep identifying the numbers. Getting the numbers for your expenses can be daunting because it can seem like so much. To make things easier and more manageable, let's break them down into bite-sized goals. Here are two suggestions on exactly how to do that.

Option One is breaking the expense groups (*Needs, Wants, Fun*) into daily tasks. Day one, you get the numbers for the *Needs* category, day two, the *Wants* category and day three, the *Fun* category. In three days, you're done – Voilà!

Option Two is for if you are short on time. Each day is dedicated to a specific amount of time, maybe a half hour to get as much done from the **Expense Information Worksheet** that you can do in the allotted time frame. The next day, you pick up where you left off and continue doing this until all the expenses have been identified and the sheet is completely filled out. You can set a timer to let you know when thirty minutes is up so you don't go over that time slot. The way things get accomplished is breaking them down into manageable goals. As the saying goes, *"How do you eat an elephant? One bite at a time."* Your money freedom is the elephant, each task is the bite. Trust me, you'll get there. Just keep following the maps I give you – these worksheets are those maps.

Celebration moment – take a pause to congratulate yourself on getting through the Expenses category! Go you! You are a warrior. You know all of the amounts and due dates for your expenses! This knowledge gives you the power to make adjustments on the figures that are no longer working for you. Now you have the tool of gratitude to transform your relationship with money by using it as a way to say thank you every time you give and receive it.

FUN TIP: Every morning, I write down 5 things I am grateful for to anchor into the energy of gratitude. What are 5 things you can list right now that you are grateful for?

Tonia's Mini Money Life Lessons

Money Fear to Power

Today I'm feeling anxious. I have a knot in the pit of my stomach. So, I invite this feeling, this knot, this anxiety to speak to me. I say, "Reveal yourself on the pages of this paper." It replies: "I'm afraid we've lived life a certain way for so long and now you are saying there is another way to be and exist with money. What if you're wrong? You're not only letting yourself down, but others that you are teaching it to as well." I know it works. Yet, I'm still afraid of niching myself into responsibilities: mortgages, rent, family, kids, that I'll become a slave to money again. The only reason why it worked was because I'm alone. Once I'm responsible for others. I'm going to fail and be the slave of money again like I was in the past. The fall is going to be so much greater. As Melissa's friend Gab said: "The higher we climb up that ladder, the larger the shadow we cast." I'm afraid to lose my freedom. I'm afraid to be sucked back into the illusion of money and its power.

As I'm writing, I can see the bullshit splattered all over it. I wasn't avoiding life. Things happen to me to support me with my journey. Finding an apartment that checked off all my "must have" criteria boxes, five times!! I'm clear on what I want and it manifests. It doesn't only exist in the form of money. It's creation that is at work here. Believing is seeing, and it's real. It's accepting that I'm crazy enough to believe that another way is possible ... that money is an expression of love and gratitude.

Money is not happiness, is not power. That money illusion is meant to keep me stuck in a fear pattern and in choosing to give my power away, I'm allowing a piece of paper to determine my worth and the worth of a human being. If someone has more money, their life is of more value? That is complete bullshit. Total bullshit. Money is not that. Money is neutral and it is just a tool for us to use.

Income Information

As a result of your perseverance, the next two stops on the Focus journey are simple and fun: it's all about the money coming in (income) and money you have (savings). Let's get going on the fifth stop: income. This is the money that comes in to your life and that's always a good time so it shall be treated as such, no matter what the amount is or the frequency in which it comes into your accounts. If you don't know what that figure is, you miss out on celebrating that money. You're not going to miss a chance to celebrate, are you!? It's an important number to know every month because you cannot direct the flow of your money without knowing what the figures are for money going out (expenses – which we figured out in the previous stage, yay!) and money coming in. This creates knowing your cash flow. So, let's get moving with finding out what your monthly income is.

Below is the **Income Information Worksheet** to support you in knowing exactly what information to identify to complete the income map. It is split into two versions, fixed and variable. The first chart is *Fixed Income* and this is for anyone who receives a set monthly paycheck and set amount. The questions you're answering here are: What is your income? Does it come in weekly, bi-weekly, monthly? What are your gross and net pay amounts?

The second chart is *Variable Income* and this is for anyone who may not have a set date to get paid and/or the amount of money changes every month. The questions you are answering here are: Are you keeping track of your income on a daily, weekly, or a monthly basis? Are you keeping track of your income at all? If you do, does it feel super confusing and hard to do? Well, there's a simple and fun way to keep track of it and that's what the below worksheet is for. You will see that the *Variable Income* section is broken down into three months, because it represents a quarter of a year to give you an accurate reading of your income activity. This way, you can take the average of the three months and come up with a monthly number for your income, solving the riddle of "I don't know what my income is every month."

Let's identify what's coming in so we can say bye-bye to "I don't know" when it comes to your income! All you have to do is fill in the blanks.

INCOME INFORMATION WORKSHEET
Fixed & Variable Income

What to Do: Gather your income information from your bank statements or paystubs and fill in the worksheet. Please use the chart that corresponds with your income, depending on if you have a fixed (set amount) or variable (amount changes) income. The goal is to identify your monthly income.

FIXED INCOME		
PAYCHECK	GROSS	NET AMOUNT
Paycheck 1	$3076	$2562.50
Paycheck 1	$3076	$2562.50
TOTAL	$6152	$5125

*To download a blank version of the income information worksheet, go to **www.toniag.com/rich-resources**

VARIABLE INCOME

MO. 1	$ IN
1	-
2	$500
3	-
4	-
5	$300
6	-
7	-
8	-
9	-
10	-
11	$1000
12	-
13	-
14	-
15	-
16	-
17	$2000
18	$250
19	-
20	-
21	$300
22	-
23	-
24	-
25	$500
26	-
27	$300
28	-
29	-
30	$250
31	-
Total	$5400

MO. 2	$ IN
1	-
2	-
3	-
4	$5000
5	-
6	-
7	-
8	-
9	$1000
10	-
11	-
12	-
13	-
14	-
15	-
16	-
17	-
18	-
19	-
20	-
21	-
22	-
23	-
24	$2000
25	-
26	-
27	-
28	-
29	-
30	-
31	-
Total	$8000

MO. 3	$ IN
1	$3000
2	-
3	-
4	-
5	-
6	-
7	-
8	-
9	-
10	-
11	$500
12	-
13	-
14	-
15	-
16	-
17	-
18	$250
19	-
20	-
21	-
22	-
23	-
24	-
25	$750
26	-
27	-
28	-
29	-
30	-
31	-
Total	$4500

Variable Income Formula:
Month 1 + Month 2 + Month 3 = 3 Month Total
3 Month Total divided by 3 (number of months) = Monthly Average
$5400 + $8000 + $4500 =**$17900**
$17900 divided by 3 = **$5966**
Monthly Average: $5966

"We learn the magical lesson that making
the most of what we have turns it into more."

– Codependent No More

For those of you with a Fixed Income, put both your gross and net pay amounts in the worksheet to be aware of what they are. Gross pay is the amount you make before taxes and deductions are taken off, and your net amount is the amount you take home after all the deductions are made. You can find this information on your paycheck. It's good to know what deductions are taken from your paycheck and this information will be listed on your paystub, so go and take a look at it. If you do not keep your paystubs, just wait for your next check. If you are on direct deposit, log into your payroll provider and they will have this information in your login account. If this option is not available to you, you can ask your employer how to obtain your paystub.

Fun Fact! Always keep your two most recent pay stubs because when purchasing a big item (for example, when buying a home or renting an apartment), you will be asked for these.

If you're an entrepreneur, freelancer, or get paid on commissions (basically, if you have an inconsistent income), use the *Variable Income* chart. It's an opportunity to turn receiving money into a game. Each time you get money in, fill in the amount you received on the day you received it. You can gather this information by logging on to your bank account or grabbing the paper statement to the bank account you make your deposits in. Once in the statement, look at the date the deposit came in and place it on this worksheet, and then do this for the previous three months. Doing this gives you the chance to celebrate the income you have coming in versus comparing it to "Is it enough to pay for all my expenses?" You will have noticed a formula on the bottom of the sheet: this is there to guide you with exactly what to do to get your monthly income figure.

Handy Tip: If you have both a set paycheck and variable income, use both charts.

Celebration moment! You completed the map of your income. You're a total rock star and doing some amazing work. To bring in some fun, remember to apply gratitude to your income. Turn it into a game and celebrate the money you have coming in when it does, and take a moment to process that income as your thank you for the work you do. It's not just money, but a thank you. Receive that thank you. Take it in, appreciate it, no matter what the amount. Great work! Let's continue now on our journey to looking at savings.

> **FUN TIP:** What money have you recently received that you can say thank you for?

Savings Information

Okay, stay with me here! We are in the last category for this stage. The sixth stop is sensational savings and oh how fun it is. We are not allowing I don't know to rob us from that experience. The questions you will be answering here are: Do you have savings? If so, do you know how much? Do you know what accounts to have, in order to save in a balanced way? Do you know what amounts to have in savings to be financially secure? Here, you are strengthening yourself by identifying your savings information. Savings are the omega and I want you to understand why they are so crucial. Your savings are what allows you to get out of survival mode by creating financial security. I'll repeat: Your savings creates financial security and wellbeing with your money! On this stop of the journey, you are building three "homes" that represent your savings accounts: Savings One, Savings Two, and Retirement.

If you do not have savings, don't allow this to get you down. You're not alone, and as a nation we are completely off balance – here's a statistic to show you how. According to a survey done by gobankingrates.com: "In 2019, 69% of respondents said they have less than half $1,000 in a savings account compared with 58% in 2018. 45% of respondents, almost half of that 69%, said they have $0 in a savings account." Hence my point is to stop judging yourself because 45% of people have no money saved at all, which shows us there is a deeper, underlying story that is running the show here. The predominant narrative in our nation's money story is scarcity and lack (I'll touch more on this in the Flow Stage). We do not educate our people in financial literacy and offer it as basic knowledge so we can thrive in society instead of surviving. The above statistic is highly demonstrative of that.

For now, your job is to be kind to yourself and celebrate that you're making the changes. It began when you picked up this book. Celebrate this, instead of bashing yourself for what you haven't done. Let go of your judgment, as it is not serving you or anyone else. Below is your **Savings Information Worksheet** to guide you in building your savings money map.

Joy Tip: Your savings creates financial security and well-being with your money.

"A gem cannot be polished without friction.
Similarly, a man or a woman cannot be perfected without trials.
Understand that challenges do not come to small people,
only to those capable of greatness."

- Dr. Michael Levry

First, you want to have a high yield savings account, Savings One. The intention is to not spend this money. Just imagine it doesn't exist for spending. In the financial world, this account is referred to as "emergency" savings. However, you are not taking that word on. Instead, you are switching it to security. You have the security of knowing that no matter what happens in your life, you have the money to feed yourself and your family, to keep a roof over their heads, money for transportation to move around, and for the utilities. That's why the aim is to have six months of your *Need*

SAVINGS INFORMATION WORKSHEET

What to Do: Check the boxes that apply to you.

- ☑ Yes, I have a savings account!

- ☐ Yes, I have a second savings account for long-term savings!

- ☐ Yes, I have a retirement account!

- ☑ Yes, I have $100 saved in Savings One.

- ☑ Yes, I have $500 saved in Savings One.

- ☑ Yes, I have $1,000 saved in Savings One (celebrate – you have now moved yourself out of the 69% to the 31% of Americans, way to go!).

- ☐ Yes, I have one month of Need Expenses saved in Savings One.

- ☐ Yes, I have three months of Need Expenses saved in Savings One.

- ☐ Yes, I have six months of Need Expenses saved in Savings One.

*To download a blank version of the savings information worksheet, go to **www.toniag.com/rich-resources**

Expenses (you can find this number on your **Expense Informa-tion Worksheet** above, under "Joy Tips," item number one) so you're creating your own bank. This removes the dependency of living paycheck-to-paycheck and feeling like you have to survive through life. This is why it's imperative to be disciplined in the habit of savings. It creates a sense of wellbeing and financial security in your life. So, anytime you have the urge to take money out of this account for shopping or to buy something that's not necessary, ask yourself this question: "Is this more important than my financial security?"

If you do not have a savings account, no worries, it's super easy to open one. You don't even have to go to a bank to do it. For those of you new to having a savings account, I strongly suggest going with a bank that has no minimum balance on the account or monthly fees to use it – most online banks offer this. Another thing about online banks that make them great for savings is that it makes impulse transferring less likely, because it takes an extra step to transfer money out. You must log into another website to transfer the money, versus being on your main checking account website and transferring the money from your savings. The website gobankingrates.com is a great resource to do research on what banks are available to you and what would fit your situation best.

The next account we want to work our way up to having, if we don't already, is a second savings account, Savings Two. The intention is to have money saved for long term spending. We're creating balance in our savings, so of course we want to have savings that we can spend. Things come up and we want to enjoy the money we are making and spend it on the things we want, guilt-free. Our Savings Two is for items we are saving up to buy like a car, vacation, or a down payment on a home, etc. It allows us to feel responsible with our finances. This removes our dependency on credit cards and accumulating debt. Cultivating the habit of saving takes us out of the mindset of buy now, pay later. It moves us into having the cash available to buy what we want.

The third savings account is Retirement. This sets up your financial security and money wellbeing for the future. The money in your Retirement Account cannot be withdrawn before a certain age (look up online what the age is because the laws can change) without getting hit with a penalty fee. That's why you have the two other savings accounts – to create balance in your savings. One account for your present financial security, one to spend on long-term things, and one for your future financial security.

There's a whole bunch of different types of retirement accounts. I'm not a financial advisor or a Certified Public Accountant (CPA), so going into details here is beyond my scope of expertise. However, if you go online there's plenty of information on what types of retirement accounts there are. Here are the most common types: traditional or "Roth IRAs" (Individual Retirement Arrangements), 401k plans, SEP (Simplified Employee Pension) plans. What I want to highlight is the difference between a Roth retirement account and a traditional retirement account because choosing between Roth and traditional has an effect on the amount of money you receive when you withdraw it, so it's worth mentioning.

A general distinction between the two – Roth versus traditional – is how they are taxed. The money you contribute to your Roth account is taxed before you contribute to it, which means when you withdraw the money, you will not be taxed on that money. This is important because the money you withdraw will be a larger sum, so you do not want to be paying taxes on it then. Whereas with traditional retirement accounts, the money you contribute is made with pre-tax dollars and you get taxed when you withdraw the money. Checking with your accountant which account works best for you is a great thing to do because there are many other variables to consider as well. I want you aware of your options and to know that you have a choice to have your retirement money grow tax-free or have it taxed when you withdraw the money. Thank you for sticking by while I mentioned that. Knowledge is power and I want you to know all that you can to support yourself in making the best decisions for your financial future. Two sources that can support you with your retirement account questions are a financial advisor and an accountant.

Fun Fact: You may have a financial advisor available to you at your workplace if you have a retirement account. Inquire about it and ask who is managing this account, and get a statement for it so you know the investments your money is in. It's your money, so please know what it is being invested in and identify the person who can help you with figuring that out. Another source to speak to is at your bank. There are financial advisors you can go and talk to in readily accessible fashion.

Celebration moment! Pause and recognize that you just finished the Focus Stage. You're reclaiming your power from money and moving towards it working for you. Incredible, job well done!! Now that you have the clarity of your money story and numbers, you can move into Stage Two, Foundation, where you will create the strategy to execute the vision you create! You will have some fun using your imagination to create the world you want to live in. From a place of clarity, not confusion, you will allow yourself to dream. What a great reward!

> **FUN TIP:** Close your eyes and imagine something you want in your dream life…

Tonia's Mini Money Life Lessons

The Micro in the Macro

The drive up to Beacon with Adam and Will was magical. The leaves were magnificent in their beautiful splendor of changing colors. The trees feel vibrant and warm. The bright orange and red of the leaves made the trees look like they were on fire. Mother Nature showed us her majesty, her abundance, and the level she can create on. On a micro level, you can see the lines within one leaf and how gracefully it changes. Effortlessly. From green to yellow to orange to red and in between these colors, an infinite number of different color tones that are yet that same color. It's an endless palate of color, no two colors the same. Zoom out, you see the leaves. All the different leaves doing the same thing, yet each in their own unique way, like we do. They're a part of the whole and still individually unique. Zoom out some more, you have a complete picture of a tree with all its vibrant colors. Representing the explosive colors of a phoenix, a fire. Growth is a series of deaths and rebirths. The leaves are going down in a blaze of glory, displaying a fantastic show. Then when you zoom out some more, you see a whole mountain painted in a velvet red wine, bright fire red, golden orange like the sun when it is setting, and yellows as luminous as the sun.

These millions of leaves all display their uniqueness and majesty. Painting a perfect picture for our eyes to witness. It's eye candy at its best and I'm taking mental pictures of it all spread throughout the mountain. A rainbow of fall colors. As soon as we opened the car door, we were hit with the smell of the clean, crisp air of the abundant trees. The sounds and the winds of being outside of the city. It seems like the air itself is expanded, opened, free, and there's more of it. The gifts of the trees, they take the poison we exhale from our bodies to give us back the air we need to breathe. The perfect example of flow and balance. All this gets done through our breath. The key to it all. Nature herself gives us the gift of life by giving us the oxygen we breathe. Yet again nurturing us, nurturing me. Mind, body, and soul. There is no end to her depth and beauty. A reflection of abundance that I and all of us are connected to. All unique leaves in the majestic canvas of the forest. We are the micro in the vast macro. How wonderful is that?

Chapter 14:
Stage Two - Foundation

Welcome to Stage Two: Foundation. Here, we dream together to bring in hope, possibility, inspiration, new beginnings, joy, happiness, ease, magic, wonder and love. This is the ground your money system will be built on. By organizing your thoughts and the numbers you identified in the Focus stage, you create a vision in your mind and a structure for your money.

Call this structure a plan, budget, strategy, design, scheme, or blueprint – whichever word resonates with you most. In this stage, this structure appears as your Organization Worksheets for the six categories: mindset, accounts, debt, expenses, income and savings. These six categories are the foundation for your money structure and what you are building your new money foundation on. Over time, this structure may change and that's super important to remember. As you begin to use the plan from the worksheets in your everyday life, you may find adjustments to make it work specifically for you. As you become an expert in your money system, you can make custom adjustments and that's okay. Flexibility is key because you are each unique and operate differently. For now, I'm sharing the blueprint I use for myself and the thousands of clients I worked with to give you a simple base to work off, and along the way you can add in your custom designs.

The key intention is to have our money working smart for us and setting up a structure to support that. Here's a story on the power of dreaming and what gets created when we move into possibility and follow the blueprint.

Kristine and Isaiah are dear friends of mine and are a part of my soul family. I've known Kristine since I was five years old. When we were twenty-one, she moved to Florida, so every year I go and visit her and Isaiah (her husband) and share what I am up to with them. On one of my visits, they shared what they wanted for their future and how far away they were from it. As soon as I heard that, I instantly went into my "anything is possible" zone and I told them I could support them in getting this future, adding that it was easier than they thought.

So there we were, driving to Orlando, off to have fun at the theme parks and I was in the back seat of the car creating a strategy for them! I was going through the six categories from the Focus stage with them and by the end of that trip, they had a game plan in the form of a structure to follow. I told them if they followed the plan, they could get what they wanted. In that moment, hanging out with my friends and helping them to organize their money, it was truly confirmed – I loved this work. This is fun for me. Getting the life you dream of is play for an adult.

In 2019, I went to visit them to celebrate their moving into a new home – their dream home. I was so excited for them! While I was there, they reminded me that it was my support that helped them get this home. I was confused, and so Isaiah shared why. Two years ago when I road tested my new system with them, I asked them what they wanted in a house and to put the thought of money to one side for the moment. I told them not to think about where they were, but about where they wanted to go and to be. I urged them to allow themselves to dream and feel what they desired for them and their family. They did, and I told them, "*Why settle for three bedrooms when you want four? Get a pool. List out everything you want!*" I told them to live, to dream. Dreaming costs nothing, so they should give themselves permission to go there!

At the time, Isaiah was experiencing heart problems and Kristine was dealing with a pulmonary embolism, so they had a lot going on. They told me I had ignited hope in them. I sparked inspiration, passion, and provided a structure to make it possible. All it took was support. They followed that blueprint and ran with it! They adjusted it as they needed to and manifested their dream life into a reality. When they were looking for houses, they got exactly what they wanted because they were clear on what they wanted. They got the house with four bedrooms, pool, and a lake outside – for the exact amount of money they wanted to spend. That's the power of getting clear on your dreams and using your vision to stay the course. We are using the same six categories from the Focus stage: mindset, accounts, debt, expenses, income and savings, to structure the information into a blueprint for you to follow.

For the Mindset category we are going to create your vision, so let's go ahead now and start dreaming.

Mindset Vision

Welcome to creating your dream life! In this stage, we create a new foundation to build your "money house" on. Here, we create a vision of what you desire for yourself in the next year. A vision includes details about what you want and where you want to go.

You must see it in your mind's eye and feel it as if it's the reality you are living, right here and right now. The important thing to anchor into is, *"How do I feel?"* Yes, a four-bedroomed house with a pool and a lake is great. We saw in the earlier story that being clear on what we want is super important, but what lies underneath that – desire – is what makes it manifest. What does this house signify to you? When seeing yourself in this magnificent home, what are you feeling? Is it security, freedom, joy, peace?

The intention here is to not get attached to the physical outcome or thing. I know it seems a little backwards, but it's true. Life will give you so much more, more than you can ever imagine or create, when you surrender and trust in it (we will touch on surrender and trust in the Flow Stage). This requires you to be detached from the vision on the material plane, but to connect to it on the emotional plane. Coming from this place is what allows you to play with life. By doing this, we become master manifestors by using our feelings. Here, I must stress that it's never about the physical object of your manifestation – remember, money is a tool and cannot buy happiness. Becoming clear on the feelings and emotions you experience when dreaming of your desired outcome brings about sustainable happiness (another topic covered in the Flow Stage). This allows you to use money as the vehicle to support you in your life. If you are not happy inside, no amount of money is going to do that for you.

Tonia's Mini Money Message
Money is a tool and cannot buy happiness.

For now, give yourself permission to dream and start by asking yourself the following question: If you were right at the end of the year, reviewing how it had gone, what things did you do that made you feel proud and what ways did you embody to obtain these things? Was it a new job? Doing something you love? Working out? Eating healthy? Being in a relationship? A feeling of complete peace? Having savings? Clarity around your finances? Financial freedom? Peace? Harmony? Love? Trusting yourself completely? Moving forward in your life with complete conviction? Happiness in your day-to-day life? Having a morning ritual for yourself? Does any of this ring your internal happiness bell?

Take fifteen minutes and allow yourself to dream and complete the Vision Exercise below. Remember, this is the tool that gives you the motivation and inspiration to take action on the plan and complete the worksheets for this money system. On my website (**www.toniag.com/rich-resources**) you can access the free audio of this exercise.

Future Vision Exercise

I want you to imagine it is January 1st of the following year. You are sitting in your most cozy spot with your favorite hot beverage, reviewing the previous year. As you're doing so, your heart is singing with joy and gratitude. You had a dynamite year. You're so proud of yourself and what you accomplished. You begin to ask yourself:

What things happened in the last year that you're grateful for?

What ways of being did you embody when you accomplished these things?

What were you feeling after you accomplished these things?

Now, take some time to write these answers down. Describe what this looked and felt like, and what ways of being you were embodying.

Bonus Action

Create an inspiration board of the life you dream of, the things you desire, and the lifestyle you want to live. Cut out as many images that will fit on an 8.5 x 11 sized sheet of paper. Choose pictures that resonate with the feeling and "beingness" of your vision.

"Beauty, power, and harmony abound in my mind."

– Phil Laut

I hope you had a pleasant dream and you can always add to this vision as you go along. Remember, it's not about the material thing, it's about the feeling; the desire underneath the material object, and your beingness. Your beingness is *"the quality, state, or condition of having existence."* It's the state you are choosing to embody in order to have all that you want. Every morning in my journal, I write: "What do I want to create today and once I do, what ways of being will I embody to have that desired outcome?" Some days I am joy, or love. Some days I am courage. Focusing on your daily beingness is how you create the life you want. "Be. Do. Have."

Celebration moment. Congratulations on getting yourself through the mindset category and get excited that you created your anchor with your vision. When it gets tough or you want to give up on the plan, because it does happen, then it's time to stop and focus on your vision. Celebrate that you created your anchor. So, let's move into the next category, where we start building your "money homes."

> **FUN TIP:** I invite you to cut out an image that represents your vision. Write on it "financial freedom" and put it in your wallet as a reminder of sticking to the money plan.

Tonia's Mini Money Life Lessons

"Really, this is what going for my dreams sounds like?"

Who am I to write this book? What new information do I have to contribute to money, a topic that has been discussed for ages! Who is going to be interested in this? How am I going to promote the book and get it out there? I'm only going to sell five books. What if it sucks? Who's going to publish it? I can't write. It's not interesting enough. My grammar sucks. It's a complicated process and difficult. I'll never finish writing it. I'm being casual about it. It should be more difficult. What if I don't finish it? What if people don't get it or understand it? I'm sharing my journey with money and vulnerable moments. What if people don't agree with my views? What if people think I'm a fraud? I'll be judged and made fun of. I don't have the discipline and drive to write a book and see the process through. What if I give up or half-ass it or it's too revealing? I am baring my soul on these pages and I feel exposed. What if people do like it and I don't like attention and fame? What if I don't like success? What if I get exactly what I want and I don't like it? What if I can't bear being in the spotlight? I'm too inconsistent.

Accounts Organization

When I was growing up, it was a lot easier to keep track of the money I spent. My bills were paid out of my checking account and for daily spending I had cash on hand. When I grew up, debit cards weren't as common. We used cash, so it was easy – when the money ran out, so did my spending. In this stage, we're bringing back simplicity because keeping things simple is what keeps things doable. We are setting up your accounts in such a way that puts fail safes in to prevent overspending, and it becomes a "rinse and repeat" process that you're not thinking about. The foundation of how your accounts are set up is pivotal because most of our accounts are set up in a disorganized way and this causes confusion with our money.

A sure way to overspend is having our debit cards connected to the account we pay our monthly bills out of. We can be responsible and budget our rent or mortgage money in our account, but then we're out using our debit cards and mindlessly swiping – before we know it, we've spent our money for rent, utilities or our credit card payments. This happens because the world is set up as a world of plastic. It encourages overspending to get what we think we want now without taking the time to actually think through what we really want. So we go through life and we swipe away, forgetting how much we're spending. Well, screw that, we're too smart to fall prey to that anymore – hence why we are formulating a responsible structure for our accounts. We do this by setting up "homes" for our money so it knows where to go, on purpose, for it to be spent. Many people resist creating a budget because they think it is limiting, but building the structure for our money is what creates the freedom.

Go back to the **Accounts Information Worksheet** from the Focus Stage and transfer the information over to this worksheet, **Accounts Organization** to find the destinations for your accounts. Welcome home, money!

Tonia's Mini Money Message
Building the structure for our money
is what creates the freedom.

ACCOUNTS ORGANIZATION WORKSHEET

What to Do: In the Focus stage we listed our accounts and noted the purpose of each account, finding that most of our accounts have multiple purposes. Below we are listing out our accounts by their purpose.

Use the information from your *Account Information Worksheet* to fill in the worksheet below.

Take notice if one of your accounts plays the role of many and if some accounts are not present.

Purpose of Account: Bill Pay

Name	Acct #	Type	APY %	Min. Balance	Fee	Balance
Bank XYZ	0567	Checking	0%	$100	$15	$500

Purpose of Account: Variable Expenses Debit Card

Name	Acct #	Type	APY %	Min. Balance	Fee	Balance
Bank XYZ	0567	Checking	0%	$100	$15	$500

Purpose of Account: Fun Debit Card

Name	Acct #	Type	APY %	Min. Balance	Fee	Balance
Bank XYZ	0567	Checking	0%	$100	$15	$500

Purpose of Account: Savings One

Name	Acct #	Type	APY %	Min. Balance	Fee	Balance
Bank XYZ	0310	Savings	.50%	$0	$0	$1300

Purpose of Account: Retirement *(currently no account)*

Name	Acct #	Type	APY %	Min. Balance	Fee	Balance
-	-	-	-	-	-	-

Purpose of Account: Savings Two *(currently no account)*

Name	Acct #	Type	APY %	Min. Balance	Fee	Balance
-	-	-	-	-	-	-

Purpose of Account: Taxes *(currently no account)*

Name	Acct #	Type	APY %	Min. Balance	Fee	Balance
-	-	-	-	-	-	-

"That's been one of my mantras – focus & simplicity.
Simple can be harder than complex: you have to work hard to
get your thinking clean to take it simple. But it's worth it in the
end because once you get there, you can move mountains."

- Steve Jobs

---

*To download a blank version of the accounts organization worksheet,
go to **www.toniag.com/rich-resources**

You will see this worksheet resembles the one you completed in the Focus stage except for on this worksheet, the *Purpose of Account* line is filled in with the designated accounts to set up for your money. Each purpose will be a new money home. Having them listed makes it easy for you to match, see what accounts you already have and also which ones you will need to set up. This will show you the actions to take for the Freedom Stage. Let's learn the different homes and new structure for your money. The names of your homes are Bill Pay (checking), Variable Expenses Debit card (checking), Fun Debit card (checking), Savings One (high-yield savings), Retirement (401k, IRA's), Savings Two and Taxes (the Taxes account is for those that are self-employed or have 1099 income). If you find yourself a little nervous because you do not have a lot of your accounts set up this way or have this many accounts, it's okay. Building something does not happen overnight and now you have the blueprint. You got this. A client of mine made a simple change of switching her debit card from her main account to its own account. This one action saved her at least $100 alone in insufficient fees since she had the clarity of how much she was spending on her debit card.

You'll notice on the worksheet, the accounts are structured the same way we grouped your expenses in the Focus stage: now you're seeing why identifying in Stage One is so important. The Bill Pay account is a checking account that pays everything that is a fixed monthly payment. The Variable Expenses Debit card account is for the items that vary in their amount from month to month. The Fun Debit card account is for all the things you do that are on the side of play and joy. Savings One is your financial security account. Then comes your Retirement account (or accounts) and Savings Two, which is for long-term savings items. Last is your Taxes. This supports you in not getting slammed come tax time, and helps you to stop falling behind in setting money aside for your taxes.

Celebration moment! You just built your money homes! Congratulations on creating the plan for your accounts. You are doing great! Now go out and do something fun for yourself. I suggest doing something that doesn't have you spending money, but instead allows you to appreciate all that you already have and all that is around you.

FUN TIP: Something I enjoy doing to be silly and get me laughing is to skip down the block. I invite you to give yourself permission to be silly!
Will you sing, dance, or skip down the block for your fun?

Debt Organization

Next, we will learn the strategy to pay down your debt so you can ease on down the road to get yourself debt free. We will cover the technical side of debt and the strategy to pay it down. Keep in mind, as you enter your debt balances it is common for it to trigger negative emotions. A lot of us have shame or guilt attached to our debt. If you find judgment creeping up, thank it and tell it to take a seat. We'll deal with these feelings in the Freedom Stage. If possible, see if you can appreciate the debt versus hating on it.

> **Tonia's Mini Money Message**
> See if you can appreciate the debt
> versus hating on it.

This money you borrowed provided you with things you needed and perhaps moments of happiness. Allow your gratefulness for these moments to overshadow any shame or guilt you may feel. The debt is there – it is simply time to clear it.

Here's an inspirational story on what happens when you choose to become responsible with your debt. A client of mine decided he was ready to take responsibility for his debt and receive the support he needed to come up with a plan to pay it off (the one I am sharing below with you all). When you have a clear vision of what you want, the universe responds. When the pain of his debt came up, he blessed it with gratitude. In 6 months, he doubled his salary and was able to pay off 1,000's of dollars in debt. That's the power of intention and a great plan. Let's get going on learning the plan to get you debt free.

I have read a lot of financial books and found that the best strategy for paying down debt is Dave Ramsey's Debt Snowball Method. The intention is to focus on paying down one specific debt at a time while staying in good standing with all your other debts by paying the minimum balances on them. Let me explain why it works. When you are paying down all your debts at the same time and putting a little extra money towards each card, you have them all decreasing at the same time and it's a slow process. It feels like nothing is happening and it's this feeling of discouragement that can cause you to stop following the plan. You yield more by paying extra money to one card and putting all your attention on that card (while still paying the minimum balances on the other cards). Being focused in this way will get things moving quicker. This is the mindset behind the snowball method. You are focusing all of your energy, attention, and money to the debt with the highest APR because that is the debt you are losing the most money to in interest.

This is all to turn money that is not working for you into money that *is* working for you. You are working smart and paying off the balance with the highest APR so your money isn't being used on interest and fees.

Before we start focusing on the account with the highest APR, we will pay off the account with the lowest balance. This way, you experience how good it feels to pay off a debt. That feeling of freedom when the balance goes to zero is exhilarating, and is a feeling you want influencing your actions. So, the debt you list first on the worksheet is the debt with the lowest balance. After that, list each debt by the highest to lowest APR. Remember when paying off your debt, slow and steady wins the race. It can take time to pay it all off, so pace yourself and continue working the strategy. The second component is what allows your debt to be paid off quicker and in a balanced way.

This second component comes from Dave Ramsey's Debt Snowball Method. When a snowball is rolling down a hill it gets bigger and bigger, and you do not have to do anything per se for the snowball to get bigger. It's using the force of momentum. He applies this concept to paying down debt. Whenever you pay down a debt, you take the amount of money you were paying to that specific card and roll it into the next debt you're paying off. This results in the second debt getting paid off faster because there's more money going toward it, and you do not feel the burden of it because the total amount you're paying towards your debt is staying the same. The individual numbers to the specific debts are changing, but the total amount you're paying towards your debt does not.

On the next page is the **Debt Organization Worksheet** to support you in building your debt free strategy.

Joy Tips:
Free yourself of the burden of debt
by appreciating the experiences it paid for.

"Gratitude can transform any situation. It alters your vibration, moving you from negative energy to positive. It's the quickest, easiest, most powerful way to effect change in your life. Just say thank you now because you know the rainbow is coming."

- Oprah Winfrey

DEBT ORGANIZATION WORKSHEET

What to Do: Reference your *Debt Information Worksheet* (pg. 87) to fill in this worksheet.

Place the debt with the lowest balance on the first row.
Place the debt with the highest APR in the second row.
Then list each debt by the second highest to lowest APR in the rest of the rows.

Creditor	APR %	Due Date	Balance	Minimum Payment	+ Extra Money	= Amount to Pay	Current Payment Method
Discover	14.99%	20th	$1850	$41	$0	$41	Acct 0567
Macy's	25.99%	13th	$5000	$158	$41 *	$199	Acct 0567
Visa	19.99%	16th	$3400	$90	$	$90	Acct 0567
Chase	14.99%	5th	$6500	$146	$	$146	Acct 0567
TOTAL			**$16750**	**$435**			

*after top debt is paid off

*To download a blank version of the debt organization worksheet, go to **www.toniag.com/rich-resources**

In this worksheet, you will see that two new columns have been added from the previous stages' worksheet for debt: the *Extra Money* and *Amount to Pay*. These provide the structure for your numbers. The *Extra Money* column is for the additional money you're paying to that debt above the minimum requirement (don't worry if you don't have money to put here, we're going to find some in the Savings Organization category). The *Amount to Pay* column is the sum of the *Minimum Payment* and *Extra Money* columns. (The first debt is the only one that extra money gets paid to. For all the debts below it, you only have to pay the minimum amounts.) For the six columns that stayed the same you can copy across the information from the **Debt Information Worksheet** in the previous stage. Since you are aware of the interest amount, there's no need to keep carrying it forward. If you didn't have a chance to fill out the details in the Focus stage, here's another opportunity to do it now. If you find yourself getting information overload, pause and breathe. Remember, clarity creates freedom. This strategy is for debt freedom.

When you pay off the top debt (yay!), cut up that credit card so you no longer use it! You don't have to close your account because it does affect your credit report, so if this is a concern, just cut it up so you can no longer use it. If you find that your minimum balances are too high for you to pay and you cannot afford them, you can use the website http://www.magnifymoney.com – it's a great website that compares the best offers for balance transfers and loans. Remember, if you do a balance transfer, you still have to make a monthly payment and you get charged a balance transfer fee. Another option is to call the company and see if you can negotiate with them, let them in on your plan and that you will pay it off and the time frame of it. You never know if you don't ask.

Working this strategy has you on the road to being debt-free! Now that you are using your debit card for fun spending, there's no reason for you to be using a credit card. If you want something, save up for it and buy it. Break the cycle of debt by changing the mindset of buy now and pay later. Reframe it to save first, buy, then fully enjoy the thing you bought in CASH! Paying for something in cash is contagious. It's knowing that the exchange is done right there in the moment – it allows for continuous joy to come through.

Celebration moment! Congratulations on using the **Debt Organization Worksheet** to support you in creating your strategy to get debt-free. Now you know the steps to take to get you out of debt, this is a big deal! Celebrate yourself on this milestone and *imagine* being free! This is exciting and fabulous. For some fun, take a moment and think about how that's going to feel. Freedom. Woweeee. Incredible work.

FUN TIP: I invite you to go outside somewhere that you enjoy or love (or even somewhere inside) and take a moment to do this imagining.

Expense Organization

Welcome to your next stop, expenses. What happens when you are no longer saying, "I don't know," and *know*, what you spend your money on? What do you do with this information? Well, you organize these expenses into three groups: Fixed, Variable and Fun so you no longer have to micromanage all of your spending. Yes to that! These expense groups get created by the account that specific bill gets paid out of, depending on if it is a set monthly payment (Bill Pay), a bill that varies – in amount and frequency – from month to month (Variable) or things you do that are enjoyable (Fun). This structure allows a mindset of conscious spending to come in, easily and effortlessly by telling your money exactly where to go and the "home" to go to. It's time to fill these accounts up with some money, intentionally! This creates order with your finances and has your money working for you! You tell it where to go and what to pay, not vice versa.

Arranging the accounts this way allows for us to find the money that was just disappearing in your accounts because of the disorder. In the next stage, we're going to find this lost money. The great part is you already figured out these numbers in the Focus stage under the *Expenses* category, so the hard work is already done. Each stage is a layer that builds on the next – they are stepping stones. You're taking the numbers from the Focus stage and transferring them into the **Expense Organization Worksheet**, in the *Amount* column. This allows you to figure out how much money is required in each account: Bill Pay checking, Variable Debit Checking and Fun Debit. This way, you are creating the money map with your expenses with this Blueprint. Let's get mapping!

EXPENSE ORGANIZATION WORKSHEET

What to Do: Take the numbers from the *Expense Information Worksheet* in the previous stage and transfer them into the worksheet below, in the Amount column.

FIXED EXPENSES GROUP

EXPENSES	AMOUNT	NEW PAYMENT METHOD
Cable TV	$120	Bill Pay Checking
Car Insurance	$100	Bill Pay Checking
Car Payment	$250	Bill Pay Checking
Cell Phone	$100	Bill Pay Checking
Donations	$50	Bill Pay Checking
Electric	$100	Bill Pay Checking
Gas	$100	Bill Pay Checking
Gym Membership	$75	Bill Pay Checking
Internet	$80	Bill Pay Checking
Total minimum debt payments	$435	Bill Pay Checking
Mortgage/Rent	$1800	Bill Pay Checking
Subscriptions	$50	Bill Pay Checking
FIXED EXPENSES Total	**$3260**	

VARIABLE EXPENSES GROUP

EXPENSES	AMOUNT	NEW PAYMENT METHOD
Gas (Car)	$60	Variable Debit Checking
Grocery	$400	Variable Debit Checking
Toiletries	$120	Variable Debit Checking
Tolls / EZ Pass	$40	Variable Debit Checking
VARIABLE EXPENSES Total	**$620**	

FUN EXPENSES GROUP

EXPENSES	AMOUNT	NEW PAYMENT METHOD
Classes / Workshops	$75	Fun Debit
Clothing	$100	Fun Debit
Entertainment	$100	Fun Debit
Gifts	$50	Fun Debit
Hair	$60	Fun Debit
Nails	$100	Fun Debit
Restaurant/Takeout	$500	Fun Debit
FUN EXPENSES Total	**$985**	

GRAND TOTAL: Fixed, Variable & Fun Expenses	$4865

*To download a blank version of the expense organization worksheet, go to **www.toniag.com/rich-resources**

Joy Tip:
BEWARE: Getting control of your money
might make you feel strong and powerful!

"What you resist, persists."

- Carl Jung

Okay, great job in entering the numbers and organizing your expenses by the account it's paid out of. Let's go through what each group is and what is in each account. This way, you know the account that each individual expense is meant to be paid out of.

The Fixed Expense Group gets paid out of your Bill Pay checking. The Bill Pay checking account is going to pay everything that is a set monthly expense. A *fixed monthly expense* is a bill that comes in every month, consistently, in the same dollar amount, such as mortgage, rent, gym and cellphone. (Some will fluctuate slightly, such as electric and gas bills but we got the three months average in the Focus Stage, so you got this covered!).

The Variable Expenses Group gets paid out of your Variable Debit Checking. This is for the items that vary in both their amount from month to month and the frequency in which you pay them. They tend to be items that are paid with a debit card or credit card, such as dry cleaning, groceries and toiletries. Some of these expenses are needs and some of them are wants, but they are definitely not fun. We want these variable expenses in a separate account so you have money for your fixed expenses and set money aside for your fun expenses.

The fun expense group gets paid out of your Fun Debit. The expenses under the "fun" group are all the things you do that are on the side of play and joy (going out to dinner, going to the movies, a day at the beach). Now, you can do these things that are fun and the money is already there. These expenses are also the ones that are easy to mindlessly swipe for and overspend. So, we go through the trouble of putting money in separate accounts to enjoy guilt-free spending! Have fun!

We just reached another celebration moment! Congratulations on using the **Expense Organization Worksheet** to support you in creating your money structure. This is massive. No longer will your money get lost – you are the captain steering your money ship. How exciting! The fun for this category is in the very fact that you have a fun account. This allows you to enjoy your spending whilst feeling responsible doing so. Bye-bye, guilt!

FUN TIP: Take a piece of paper and write down three things you are excited to spend your fun money on. Feel the joy that this simple act brings!

Income Organization

Just like it was super important to organize your expenses by figuring out where they get paid out of, we are going to do the same with your income. If you don't tell your income where to go, how will you have the money to spend on your expenses? This is exactly why you are filling in the amounts below, so you know the amount of income to transfer to each bank account. This creates organization with your income. Since all incomes are not created equal, we've broken it down into two groups: fixed and variable. This means that all income types are represented.

Here's a fun fact – a client of mine who I did this process with was able to save $9,000 in 3 years by telling her income (that was just getting lost in her expenses) where to go.

There are two worksheets (fixed and variable) to organize your income information and guide you on the actions to take when you get paid. These figures represent the amount of money to transfer every month for your income so you are directing the flow of your money. First is the **Fixed Income Organization Worksheet** for those of you with a fixed income, i.e., salaried employees whose paycheck is the same amount each month.

———————————

"The great arises out of small things that are honored and cared for. Everybody's life really consists of small things."

– Eckhart Tolle, A New Earth

———————————

FIXED INCOME ORGANIZATION WORKSHEET

What to Do: From your **Income Information Worksheet**, fill in the amount of your net income into the middle box.

From your **Expense Organization Worksheet**, fill in the total amounts for the left three boxes.

The right three boxes will be figured out in the next category, Savings.

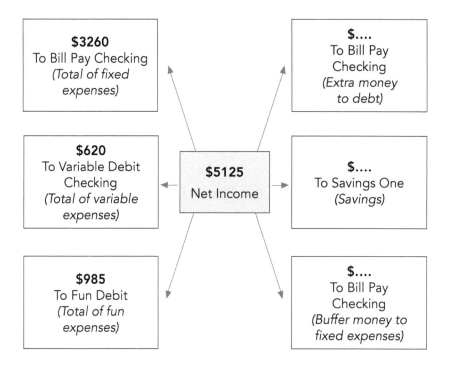

*To download a blank version of the fixed income organization worksheet, go to **www.toniag.com/rich-resources***

The left three boxes represent the expense groups: *fixed, variable* and *fun* (which we've discussed in the Expense category). The right three boxes represent the groups *extra money to debt, Savings One*, and *buffer money to fixed expenses*. Since we are introducing three new groups, I want to elaborate further on these transfers and what they do.

Extra money to debt is the money we designate to our top debt, in addition to the total minimum balance amount we are paying. This way we pay off our debt faster. If you have no debt, then no money goes here. Savings One is the amount we pay ourselves for the income we work so damn hard for and deserve to keep for ourselves. The *buffer money to fixed expenses* is money that we keep in our Bill Pay checking account for those bills that can just pop up. This way we pad the account knowing that random things do happen – actually, we plan for it! Each box tells us the amount to transfer, the account to transfer it to and in parenthesis, the purpose of the transfer.

At the top of each box by the dollar symbol, you are entering the total amount for *fixed, variable* and *fun* expenses from the **Expense Organization Worksheet**. For the right three boxes, you are calculating these amounts in the next category on the **Savings Organization Worksheet**.

In the middle of the box is the name of the account to transfer that money to. This tells you the home your money is going to and creates your road map on what to do each month with your money. All your money is accounted for and working for you. In the center box is your *Net Income* that we identified on your **Income Information Worksheet**. We use your net amount because that is the amount of money that hits your bank account when you get paid. You can split the transfer amounts according to the way your paycheck gets given to you. If you are paid weekly, then you divide each transfer amount by four. If you are bi-monthly or every other week, divide by two. Voilà! A plan for your income.

I know there's a big portion of you who don't receive your income by a consistent paycheck or a fixed amount: freelancers, entrepreneurs and commission-based salaries, to name some. It may feel at times the inconsistency is a burden and the reason why a budget can never be set up, but that's just another limiting story. Breaking out your transfers allows you to eliminate that story. The gift of an inconsistent income is you have the means to make more if you want. The question is, where does this "more" money go to when you make it? That's why there is an extra step for you. Our goal is to create a structure for your income inconsistency. Now that you know your *fixed* and *variable* expenses, you will naturally focus on putting your income to those accounts first, as they are a priority. Once you have satisfied your *fixed* and *variable* expenses you will break out your remaining income into six categories, by percentages.

Breaking out your money by a percentage is a beautiful thing because it allows for consistency and balance with your money. No matter what the amount is, it gets split into six groups, so all your accounts are growing in money at the same time. A huge complaint I hear when working with my inconsistent income clients is that they fall behind on their taxes. Well, not anymore, you have a transfer for that. The six transfer groups change depending on whether you have debt or not. The reason you still see a transfer going to your fixed and variable expense accounts is because you want to build a cushion for the months the income may slow up.

Tonia's Mini Money Message
The gift of an inconsistent income is you have the means to make more if you want.

Complete the **Variable Income Organization Worksheet**, either using with or without debt, depending on your circumstances.

"What you seek, is seeking you."

– Rumi

What to Do: Go to your **Expense Organization Worksheet** and take your fixed and variable expense amounts and fill them in the boxes below (priority 1 and 2).

Priority 1 – Transfer your income as it comes in into this designated account until you fulfill the amount of your total fixed expenses in the box below. Then move to Priority 2.

$3260
To Bill Pay Checking
(Total of fixed expenses)

Priority 2 – Transfer the rest of your income as it comes in into this designated account until you fulfill the amount of your total variable expenses in the box below. Then move to Priority 3.

$620
To Variable Debit Checking
(Total of variable expenses)

Priority 3 – Once priority 1 and 2 are satisfied, transfer all remaining income as instructed in the next table. You can transfer this money at the end of each week, do not wait. We don't want you to lose money.

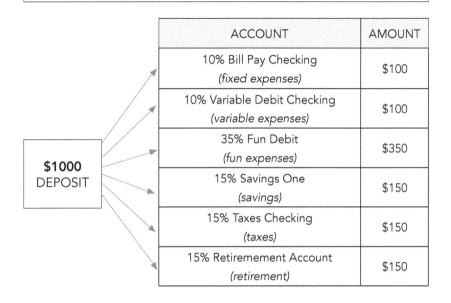

NO DEBT

	ACCOUNT	AMOUNT
	10% Bill Pay Checking (fixed expenses)	$100
	10% Variable Debit Checking (variable expenses)	$100
	35% Fun Debit (fun expenses)	$350
	15% Savings One (savings)	$150
	15% Taxes Checking (taxes)	$150
	15% Retiremement Account (retirement)	$150

$1000 DEPOSIT

WITH DEBT

	ACCOUNT	AMOUNT
	10% Bill Pay Checking (fixed expenses)	$100
	10% Variable Debit Checking (variable expenses)	$100
	35% Fun Debit (fun expenses)	$350
	10% Savings One (savings)	$100
	15% Taxes Checking (taxes)	$150
	20% Bill Pay Checking (extra debt money)	$200

$1000 DEPOSIT

*To download a blank version of the variable income organization worksheet, go to **www.toniag.com/rich-resources**

For priority number three, I suggest transferring your income at the end of each week. You total up your deposits for that week and transfer them out to their six categories. This way your money doesn't get lost in your main account before you can transfer it.

All the percentages equal up to 100%, allowing all of your money to go somewhere. No matter what the amount, these six categories will always get filled every time you get paid. That's the art of money balance. Once your debt is paid off, the 20% that was going towards your debt gets broken down into your savings – specifically, your Retirement account. The percentages breakout creates a well-balanced distribution for your money. It solves the problem of not being able to create a structure because of inconsistent income!

Celebration moment! Congratulations on using the **Income Organization Worksheets** and using the formulas to support you in creating a money structure for your income! This is tremendous. No longer will your money just go to expenses and not to you. You are creating money balance with all your money. I am so very proud of you. I invite you to go out and do something fun for yourself that doesn't cost anything, but allows you to appreciate all that you already have. Use your imagination…

> **FUN TIP:** Something I love to do that makes me feel expansive is going for a walk by water. Where can you go to allow yourself to take in the beauty of nature?

Tonia's Mini Money Life Lessons

Stuck in Flow

I'm desiring structure and I'm struggling with allowing the masculine to come in and support me. To support me in creating my vision because I now have the clarity. I've gone through the stages of manifestation and now it is time for action (cue in Redman song), but I want to stay stuck in flow. I'm trying to allow myself to be truly fluid by not getting attached to my surroundings, routines and processes. To favor my masculine or feminine energy and going with what my body truly needs, but I'm afraid of my "controller/masculine" self and I'm shaming it.

The woman who loves structure, order, schedules and getting things done no matter what. I am afraid of my robotic self. The one who will choose to complete things on a to-do list over fun and connection. The one who can stay hiding and stuck behind the lists and organizing. I am not her anymore. Yes, she is still me, but we have evolved. So, I do not have to shame this version of myself that I was in the past. I welcome her into the process and invite her in as a great support to the journey, knowing I can balance between the two. Harmony is balancing and allowing the masculine and feminine to dance. I chose to dance.

Savings Organization

Welcome to category six, savings. A good rule of thumb is to save 10% of all you earn. If you earn $5,000 a month, saving $500 a month is a good amount. However, the problem I've found with such a general rule is that some people are not able to save that much money. So I have created a strategy to help you find a healthy number for you to start saving every month. You are choosing what fits for you and your way of life. Right now, it's not so much about the amount to save than it is to start saving! The intention is to cultivate the habit of savings, nurture it and then tend to it consistently.

So often we judge our income by the expenses going out, that we forget to appreciate the money we have coming in and even worse, forget to pay ourselves! This is now changing. A portion of all the money you make gets paid to you! Pause and take that in. You work hard for your money and deserve to keep the money you earn. Your savings is where you store this money and pay yourself.

We are using the **Savings Organization Worksheet** to figure out this amount by calculating the money remaining in our account after we pay all of our expenses. Normally, this money would just blend in with the rest of the money in our account. Well, not anymore. Time to shine, remaining money, and go to our savings! If you have some stuff coming up right now because *you never have money remaining at the end of the month,* I got you. Scenario Three in this category will cover that. Till then, love up on the income you have currently coming in.

Tonia's Mini Money Message
A portion of all the money you make
gets paid to you!

SAVINGS ORGANIZATION WORKSHEET

What to Do: If you have a fixed income enter your *Net Amount*. If you have a variable income enter your *Average Monthly Amount*.

The directions column will guide you on which worksheets to find the amounts needed.

ITEM	NET AMOUNT	AVERAGE MONTHLY AMOUNT	DIRECTIONS
	(Fixed)	(Variable)	
Income	$5125	$5970	On Income Information Worksheet (pg. 103)
subtract	-	-	
Total of Expenses	$4865	$4865	On Expense Organization Worksheet, (pg. 136) Grand Total number.
Total Remaining Amount	**$260**	**$1105**	

*To download a blank version of the savings organization worksheet, go to **www.toniag.com/rich-resources**

"Life will be a party for you, a grand festival, because life is the moment we're living right now."

– Paulo Coelho, *The Alchemist*

On this worksheet, we want to focus on the *Total Remaining Amount* of your income aka *found money*. This was the amount of money getting lost in your account every month. You were being reactive with your money and putting it to wherever it was needed to at that moment. Well, bye-bye to that, because you are being proactive, not reactive. Now, you can intentionally put this money to work in your bank accounts instead of continuing to allow it to get lost. Since life situations aren't so cookie cutter, at the end of the month you may find yourself not have money remaining. If this is you, I got you. From years of working with many clients, I have found that when it comes to finding additional money after paying expenses, people typically fall into three scenarios.

> **Tonia's Mini Money Message**
> You are being proactive, not reactive.

Scenario One: You have money remaining (aka found money) and have no debt.

Scenario Two: You have money remaining (aka found money) and have debt to pay off.

Scenario Three: You are short on money every month or break even. We're going to find you some money.

You may find that in time your situation moves into another one of these scenarios.

For those with a *variable income*, the **Variable Income Organization Worksheet** gave you the strategy for your remaining money, with the percentage groups (Priority Three).

If you find you are short money every month or break even, read through Scenario Three to help you find some lost money.

Scenario One: You have money remaining and have no debt. You are designating the found money to your savings and a small amount (a buffer amount) to your Bill Pay checking account. You are designating 80% of the found money to your Savings One and 20% to your Bill Pay checking as a buffer for the unexpected bills that pop up, because they always do. I have found that typically 20% of the remaining amount is what my clients need as a buffer in their Bill Pay checking. This money was getting lost every month and going wherever it wanted, now you are intentionally putting it to work in your accounts. Congratulations, you are now saving and paying yourself first!

Scenario Two: You have money remaining and have debt. In this scenario, you have one more step and it's to support you in paying down your debt quicker. Yay to that! You are designating 60% of the found money to your Savings One, 20% to your Bill Pay checking as a buffer, and 20% to your debt, as extra money to pay your top debt. The one you are laser focused on to pay off first. It will be tempting to send more of this found money to your debt, but remember, a portion of all you earn is yours to keep. You are worth it, save it!

SAVINGS ORGANIZATION SCENARIOS

Scenario One: You have a *Total Remaining Amount* and no debt. Formula:

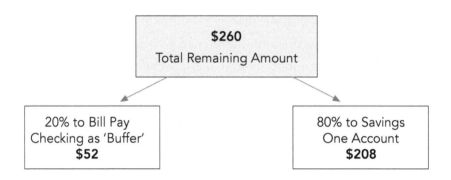

Scenario Two: You have a *Total Remaining Amount* and you have debt. Formula:

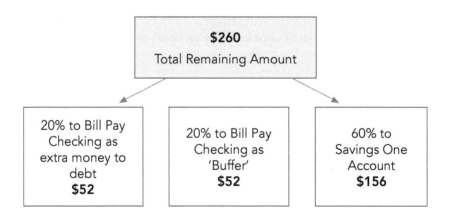

*To download a blank version of the savings organization scenarios, go to **www.toniag.com/rich-resources**

Scenario Three: This is for those of you that have no money remaining or are short of money at the end of each month. Don't worry, I'm a money whisperer and we are going to find some money for you. Through all my years of doing this work, there are a few things we tend to overspend on: transportation and food, especially now in the era of Ubers, Lyfts, Seamless and Fresh Direct. If you're taking Ubers or Lyfts and are not saving, it's time to take public transportation instead. Cut that out or cut it back, because this comfort is costing you your financial peace of mind and not allowing you to keep a portion of all you earn for yourself!

Food is another expense that's so easy to overspend on. Let me show you how you can find some lost money here. Let's take our daily coffee, for example (if you do not drink coffee, substitute it for the thing you buy to drink daily). Let's say you get coffee every day and you spend $5 on this item. If we break it down, $5 spent seven days a week is a total of $35. $35 a week becomes $140 a month. Which means you are spending $1,680 a year on coffee – money that could instead be going to your savings. It's the baby steps that have the greatest impact, and it starts with you taking ownership of your choices. No longer deciding to sacrifice your peace of mind and security by unconscious spending. It's time to exchange one for the other. Money freedom awaits! If you're worried about just cutting back on expenses, please don't, in the

Flow stage we will talk about ways to increase your income not just cut back on expenses.

I have a fun experiment for you to do. Take a look at the expenses in the "fun" and "want" groups on the **Expense Information Worksheet.** This time, take a closer look and find items you could live without. It may not always be comfortable but there is always money there, I can assure you. I know, I know, we all love to go out to eat, I get it! The harsh truth is, there is found money hidden in your expenses but it's uncomfortable to go looking for it. I've had so many clients come back to me, in shock, that they found money and how unconsciously and automatically they were spending it. One client realized she was spending $75 a week on cigarettes. Not only was she was able to start saving $300 a month (that's $3,600 a year!) but she stopped a bad habit.

As you are going through your expenses and looking for things to cut back on, you may ask yourself, "How much money am I looking for?" If you are short every month and you want to start saving, you are looking for these amounts. For instance, if you are short $200 a month and you want to start saving $50 a month, you are looking for $250. If you break even every month, come up with how much you want to save and find that amount. Go to your **Expense Information Worksheet** from the Focus stage and review your "fun" and "wants" expenses – see what you can cut back on in these groups. As you're finding ways to cut your expenses, make sure you continue to update your expense worksheets.

Now, that you have found money and have a Total Remaining Amount, go back to scenarios 1 and 2 from this category and follow the scenario that suits your situation. Do you realize that once you break out the amount to your savings, you will create the roadmap for your income to travel on each month? Voilà, order and balance with your money!

Celebration time! You completed the Foundation stage! You are close to halfway through – go you! You are building a strong, sound foundation and you have a plan for all of the six main money categories to support that foundation. This is incredible – how long have you been saying you want a plan for your money, and now you have it! Hey, in this category you even figured out how to keep a portion of all you earn! Let's bring in some fun to celebrate. Allow yourself to be silly or do something you loved to do as a child. Go ahead, treat yourself to that innocent fun.

> **FUN TIP:** Something that is easy and always makes me smile are bubbles. For some fun, go out, get some bubbles, and let your inner kid run wild!

Chapter 15:
Stage Three - Freedom

Welcome to the third stage, Freedom. On this stop on the journey, you are shifting into a new mentality with your money, intentional living and conscious spending! You are liberating yourself from the illusion of money and the power it holds. You're stepping into inspired action to create a life that excites you and lights you up. You are the driver of your money vehicle. Here, you are creating an empowering language to support you in manifesting your vision through inspired action, and getting clear on the steps to form your new money habits.

> **Tonia's Mini Money Message**
> You are the driver of your money vehicle.

You are inviting the emotions surrounding money to arise from your unconscious so they are in your awareness. When the money stories like, *"I don't know"* are gone and you have clarity around your numbers, space is created within your body and from that space your emotions emerge. These money emotions fuel your actions and reveal themselves through the actions you do and do not take. That's why we have Action Worksheets in this stage, so we can reclaim our power and truth. You are allowing your money emotions to present themselves. Here's an example of how it may show up:

> *You know it's in your best interests to open up your Variable Debit Checking, but you just haven't done it yet. The excuses of "I don't have the time" or "I'm too busy" get in the way. You haven't started saving money. The excuse of "something more important popped up" for you to spend your money on gets in the way.*

Why does this keep happening? What's the reason you're not doing things for yourself? The answer is your money pain, your emotions. Thoughts of unworthiness, shame, guilt, not being enough, scarcity, desperation, and so much more. Here, you are creating freedom from the thing really controlling your money – your emotions. You invite these emotions to reveal themselves to you so you can listen, release them, and put new thoughts in place by using the power of your words. We get clear on the actions to take for the six categories (Mindset, Accounts, Debt, Expenses, Income and Savings Action) to establish new healthy money habits. New habits get created from the repetition of our actions.

Tonia's Mini Money Message
You are creating freedom from the thing really
controlling your money – your emotions.

This stage is about having clarity on the steps to take, therefore paving the way for whatever limiting beliefs are standing in the way of you stepping into your money power. Every time a belief comes up that no longer serves you, I want you to imagine yourself clicking off a box to "unsubscribe" to that belief, just like you do when you no longer want to receive an email. It's "unsubscribing time" from the old money conditioning. You are cleaning out your mental inbox and subscribing to money being an expression of love and gratitude. You are subscribing to money being a way for you to say thank you in your everyday life! You are subscribing to money being pleasurable and fun.

High vibes attract high vibes, so you want to stay in the energy of joy, love, and freedom, which all carry a high vibration. When our energy is coming from this place of high energy, we start to attract what we desire. It allows the word "ease" to come into our lives and support us. You'll hear, *"I'm a money magnet"* and *"I'm a master money manifestor,"* and so forth. You may wonder, *"How does this happen? How can I become a money magnet?"* This is exactly what we are learning in this stage, so let's find out the actions we take in the six categories mentioned above. This way, we can get some ease and freedom around our money!

Mindset: *Empowering Language and Emotional Intelligence*

In Stage One (Focus), we built our empowering money story. In Stage Two (Foundation) we built an empowering vision. Here, we are taking it one step further by working with the words we use in our everyday vocabulary to build an empowering language. Afterwards, you will start to view your emotions as a potent tool, by learning to decode them to reclaim truths within yourself.

Welcome, let us begin your freedom journey by being intentional with the power of our words and identifying those that are limiting to your growth. The words we speak influence our actions, therefore let's start viewing our words as the commands our brains give us on what to do. Imagine a person who keeps saying "*I can't*" in their daily language while trying to form new habits: "*I can't get to the bank right now to open up my new account. I can't save money, there's not enough.*" If our words are the commands to our actions, what reality do you think "*I can't*" will create? The reality of not doing the things you desire to do. So, we are removing "*I can't*" from our vocabulary.

Another phrase that's a great indicator of something you are just doing because of old conditioning is, "*I should.*" For example, "*I should be saving.*" Why? Who said so? If your intention is to save, get clear on it. "*I am saving my money.*" Whenever you hear yourself saying "*I should,*" check in with yourself to make sure it is something you want to be doing and not some old rules you subscribed to. Remember, you have the power to unsubscribe to the rules, thoughts and beliefs that no longer serve you. Let's begin reviewing the **Empowering Money Language Worksheet** to assist you with being intentional with your words and conscious in your actions.

The brain is no longer a record of the past but a map to the future."

– *The Art of Loving*, Joe Dispenza

EMPOWERING MONEY LANGUAGE

Empowering Language Tips:

- Speak from a place of "*I.*" Claim your experience versus being general and saying "*you.*"
- Speak in the present tense, as if it is so! Remember, the now is the only reality that actually exists.
- Release the concept of form and time – the "how."

Disempowering Phrases:

- Absolutes like "*never*" and "*always.*"
- "*I'll try.*" Yoda said it best to Luke Skywalker: "*Do or do not. There is no try.*"
- "*I have to*"
- "*I should*"
- "*I can't*"
- "*I don't have*"
- "*I will not*"

Empowering Phrases:

- "*I choose to _____*"
- "*I intend to _____*"
- "*I will _____*"
- "*It's important to me to _____*"

Examples:

I'll try to save money.
Changes to: *I will save money.*

I should follow my money plan.
Changes to: *I intend to follow my money plan.*

I can't make more money.
Changes to: *I will make more money.*

I have to pay off my debt.
Changes to: *It's important to me to pay off my debt.*

I don't have savings.
Changes to: *I choose to save.*

*To download a blank version of the empowering money language sheet, go to **www.toniag.com/rich-resources**

You are now being conscious of the words and sentences coming out of your mouth. If you find yourself using disempowering phrases, switch them to those that are empowering. Above, I listed examples on how to do that with situations pertaining to your money. Instead of *trying* to save, you *will* save. As mentioned above, Yoda said it best with "*Do or do not. There is no try.*" Trying is a poor attempt, whereas saying you WILL declares that you're making a commitment to the action. Play around with these phrases. Practice saying them out loud and if you want to go deeper, practice saying them in the mirror. If you like to be held accountable, share this worksheet with a friend or partner and ask them to point out if they hear you using any words that are disempowering (in the Fun stage, we will get more into the power of community and using a journey partner to support you in your growth).

Another thing you could do to support you in learning the language is taking a picture of the sheet to keep on your phone. This way, if you catch yourself saying a disempowering phrase, you can simply replace it with an empowering one. The best thing to do is correct yourself the moment it is happening because one thing is for damn sure – as long as you say you can't, you won't be able to achieve the thing or task you want. Therefore, cut that crap out immediately!! You deserve better than that and I will not allow you to treat yourself that way. You're too special. Remember, we are embracing the mantra of *intentional living, conscious spending*.

Next, let's find the gift in our emotions. We are inviting our emotions in so we can understand the message they have for us. Being emotional and owning our emotions has never been a thing we were taught to embrace. Actually, the common message out there (especially for women) is that being too emotional is bad and not good. Men get it too, though: *"Men don't cry,"* or *"Don't be a girl."* For men, they are trapped in the message that it is wrong to show any emotion, so it may require more of an effort to get in touch with their emotions. How many times have you heard the words, *"Stop being so emotional!"* or *"Don't show your emotions!"* Patriarchy is at work here.

Instead of feeling, we "should" push our emotions to the side or bury them deep down inside of us. Well, F that! Not anymore. It is possible for all of us to change this, irrespective of how we identify ourselves; it's a collective shift in attitudes that we are striving towards. When we understand our emotions and do not shame them, we reclaim our power from our subconscious. To gain freedom, we are choosing to release our shame around our emotions and embracing them. The only thing burying and shaming our emotions does is make them stronger. Freedom comes when we shift our perspective from judgment to acceptance. Throughout this section, I am giving you the tools to do so.

It's time to restore the integrity of our emotions and unveil the truth of money. It's not just therapists and financial advisors who are authorized to be experts in emotions and money. It's time to become our own financial therapists, so money is no longer used as a way to manipulate and control. Our emotions are the main target for the marketing magicians. Billions and billions of dollars get spent on this to target you and your emotions. Do any of these sound familiar?

This thing or product will fix your problem!
This car will bring you this status!
These sneakers will make you jump higher!
These clothes will make you cool!
This house makes you look successful!
Emotions + marketing = manipulation

Guess what, people: ***nothing external will ever make you happy.*** Only you can do that for yourself. Learning mastery over your own emotions is the way out of being manipulated. You now control where to put your money (with your money homes/ accounts) and what you want to spend it on. True freedom lies in embracing and understanding our emotions. The first tool we are using is the Abraham-Hicks Emotional Guidance Scale.

The only thing wrong with our emotions and feelings is not understanding them, and so we need to learn how to empower ourselves around them. In the book *Ask and It Is Given* by Esther and Jerry Hicks, Abraham explains twenty-two of the most common emotions and how each one holds a certain vibration of either "high" or "low." We can want to attract the good, the joy, the love – and yet when interacting with others in everyday life, we can be angry, worried and overwhelmed. When we are angry, worried and overwhelmed, those are the experiences we are inviting into our lives. So, it's not enough to say we want the good in our lives; we must embody it in order to attract it. See the importance of being aware of your emotions? We want to embody the high-vibe emotions and in order to do that, we first must know which emotions those are.

On the next page is the **Emotional Thermometer** based on the Abraham-Hicks Emotional Scale. We are using this tool to learn what your emotional temperature is and how to take it. The emotions are listed from high vibration to low vibration.

––––––––––––––––

"Just as there is a health warning on every package of cigarettes, perhaps there should be similar warnings on every bank note & bank statement. 'Money can activate the pain-body & cause complete unconsciousness.' "

– Eckhart Tolle, *A New Earth*

––––––––––––––––

EMOTIONAL THERMOMETER

What to Do: Every day, ask yourself, Are my words and actions anchored in high or low vibe emotion? Use the below thermometer to see what emotion you are feeling so you can read what your emotional temperature is.

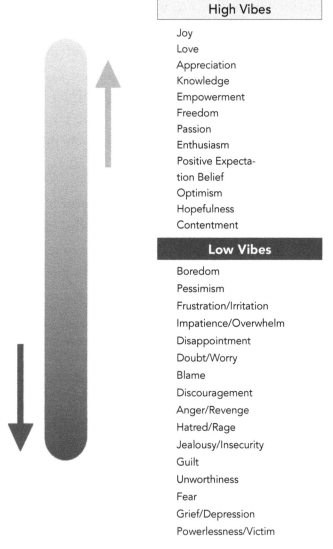

High Vibes
Joy
Love
Appreciation
Knowledge
Empowerment
Freedom
Passion
Enthusiasm
Positive Expecta-
tion Belief
Optimism
Hopefulness
Contentment

Low Vibes
Boredom
Pessimism
Frustration/Irritation
Impatience/Overwhelm
Disappointment
Doubt/Worry
Blame
Discouragement
Anger/Revenge
Hatred/Rage
Jealousy/Insecurity
Guilt
Unworthiness
Fear
Grief/Depression
Powerlessness/Victim

*To download a blank version of the emotional thermometer worksheet, go to **www.toniag.com/rich-resources**

The reason you hear the phrase *"misery enjoys company"* is because it does. What we want to do is shift into *"joy enjoys company,"* because it does! Every day, ask yourself whether your words and actions are anchored in a higher-vibe emotion or a lower-vibe emotion. You can use the emotional thermometer to tell you this. For example, you find yourself worried if you'll have enough money this month to pay all your bills. You look at the emotional thermometer and see worry is a low-vibe emotion. The goal is to raise your vibration into a high-vibe one. What things can you do to get yourself to contentment or joy?

First, acknowledge where you are at and feel that emotion fully. This will help you naturally move through it. By identifying what you are feeling, you bring into your awareness that which allows you to start releasing it. Remember, you don't want to shove these emotions down. Second, in the Flow and Fun stages, I have a bunch of tools for you to digest, process and raise your vibration! So don't worry, I got you. Haven't you noticed at the end of each category there's been a **Fun Tip**? This has you already practicing creating your own joy, therefore raising your vibration. When you give from joy, you get back with joy!

Another amazing tool I discovered on my journey is in Phil Laut's book, *Money is My Friend*. It truly blew my mind the way he connected our emotions to money and how he laid it out so simply. I am a big believer in simplicity and the KISS principle: Keep It Simple, Sexy. Laut breaks down the emotion in the context of our relationship with money, and in the book, he lists it out as negative emotion (anger, fear, jealousy, guilt, lust and apathy, to a name a few), its meaning, its remedy, and an affirmation for it.

Let me give you an example of how I use Laut's chart in my everyday life.

> *I am paying my bills and getting angry at how little my income is this month. I go down the rabbit hole thinking, "Why is it always so inconsistent, what am I doing wrong," etc. I catch myself spiraling downward and instead of judging it and making up all these limiting stories, I go to the chart in Laut's book and look up the meaning of anger when it comes to money. Its definition is "intention contaminated with the idea of helplessness."*

> *It supports me to understand that underneath the anger, the emotion I'm covering is helplessness. What am I feeling helpless about? My income. Okay, great. Next, I look to see what the remedy is and find that it is forgiveness. I look at the affirmation, it says: "I forgive myself for not receiving what I want."*

This process helps me uncover that I'm not angry with my income – I feel helpless because I'm not receiving what I want. I sit and accept that's where I'm at and I feel the emotions coming up. I allow the sadness and disappointment of not showing up for myself to rise up in me. I feel it fully and I do not squash it or push it down. What's important is that I allowed the emotion to come through instead of shaming it because continuing to feel angry and beating myself up isn't going to do anything except keep me in the state I'm in and lower my vibration. By accepting the emotion, I allow it to tell me the truth of the story going on inside of me. This is why I call the chart the "money emotions decoder." I thank the anger for showing me what was underneath the emotion and thank Laut for his chart. To move on from this experience I used another tool – forgiveness – to complete the cycle of this emotion. Bringing us to our next tool, forgiveness.

I learned about forgiveness from two worksheets I received while taking a course given by Pastor Greg Stamper at the Celebration Spiritual Center I go to in Brooklyn. Who would have thought that an understanding about forgiveness would come in the form of two PDFs?! Before these worksheets, I had a misunderstanding of what forgiveness was and the power of it. In school, I was taught it's something I say to another person after they hurt me and apologized for it. Forgiveness was for them, but I couldn't understand why after I said, "I forgive you," I still felt anger or resentment towards that person. Just saying it wasn't enough and I didn't know there were more actions to take in order to release it fully. These sheets provided just that; it took us through the six steps to truly move through all the stages of forgiveness and shift into a new perspective (the sheets were developed by Colin Tipping, and in the *Resources* section of this book for you to use). I realized that the gift in forgiveness is that it releases you from the emotional prison you set up for yourself. Forgiveness is a tool for you to use to create freedom and peace for yourself.

Using the tools of empowered language, taking your emotional temperature, decoding your emotions and learning to forgive is crucial. The benefits are endless. One of the many benefits is that you'll begin listen to yourself more than the outside world. No longer allowing yourself to be vulnerable to consumerism and manipulated by marketing techniques that promise you happiness from products that will never deliver. Being self-aware creates freedom in your life! You are free to make choices in creating the life you really desire.

Celebration moment! You have made it through the Mindset category, where you learned about having an empowering language and using your emotions as a tool to reclaim your truth. Celebrate yourself for the tools you learned and now have in the toolkit. Now it's time for some fun. I want you to be gentle with yourself after working on your emotions – its deep work. Put some nice calm music on and do something that is relaxing for you. A nap, a bath, a warm shower or cozy up on your couch.

FUN TIP: Something I enjoy doing to relax is taking a bath. To add some extra love, I put some rose petals in and light some candles. I put a spa playlist on from Spotify and chill. What relaxing thing will you do for yourself?

Tonia's Mini Money Life Lessons

A Conversation with Fear

My discomfort stems from me shaming my fear. Once I did a spring clean (a tool I learned from Mama Gena's School of Womanly Arts) on it and gave it a voice, it was very freeing and revealing. These are real concerns and it is okay for me to voice them. It feels good to move towards them instead of pulling away. It's giving my fear a seat at the table. It just wants a voice, and it feels good to grant it that and then put it away. Make friends with my fear so I know what it sounds like when it shows up again. Once I hear it, I thank it and tell it to take a side seat because I got this. Tell fear: *"Thank you for your input, I know you meant well."* Shower it with love. Fear just wants to be heard. Own the fear that exists instead of shaming it. If I allow myself to listen to it, it just may bring me some truth, insight, vulnerability, and humility.

Tonia's Mini Money Message
Give your fear a seat at the table.

Yesterday, I experienced that with my money and my power. Am I that powerful that I attracted my partner, dream job, money, etc.? Can I really do this? Fuck yes I can. Yesterday I was living in fear, and something happened after I spring cleaned on it with my sister goddess Zoe. It's like the thermometer was lowered and the temperature of fear went down. The temper tantrum stopped. Fear didn't care if I acted on it or did anything with it – it just wanted to be heard. Once I did, it released its control and hold over me. So don't ignore it, push through it or say you're fearless because that's a fucking lie!! Fear never goes away. It actually serves a purpose for extreme situations by telling us something may be wrong.

The intention is to make friends with your fear. Listen to what it has to say. Whatever it is, listen to it and here's the big one: DO NOT SHAME IT. Learn its voice because you are going to have conversations with it and you want to be familiar with what your fear voice sounds like. Ask it: "*Okay, fear – what do you want to say to me?*" It replies ...

> "*You're a fraud, no one is ever going to listen to you as a money expert.*"
> "*You're too young to be teaching this.*"
> "*You didn't go to school for this, you're not qualified to be an expert and on money nonetheless.*"
> "*You can't make the money you want without killing yourself and working hard.*"

Well look at that. I don't judge it or attach anything to it. I listen to it and then I say to my fear dialogue or ego: "*Thank you for your concern and insight. I know you are just trying to protect me, but we got this. I can handle this and I appreciate your voice.*" Imagine it like a navigation system that's telling you to turn when there's a body of water next to you, and if you do turn, you'll fall right off the bridge. You know better than to listen to the navigation. Well, this is how you are meant to treat fear. Thank it and move on. When it comes to money, a lot of fear stories and emotions come up. It's the usual suspects of shame, guilt, worry, doubt and confusion. As you continue to grow, there will always be a new wall to climb over and conquer. So get familiar with the fear voice because you are up to big things. When it shows up, say, "*Hello, old friend,*" listen to it, thank it, and then walk away. You got this.

Accounts Actions

Welcome to category two – Accounts Actions! Here, you are setting up your money homes by making sure you have all your checking and saving accounts open so they can receive the money you mapped out from the worksheets in the previous stage. It goes back to the analogy of your money being lost if it doesn't have a map, and what's the point of a map if there is no destination? Your accounts are the destination for your money, so let's be clear on the actions to take to bring this money structure to life.

It's possible to find yourself getting stuck on what specific actions to take, or in taking the actions required. Here, beware of saying things like, *"I don't have the time,"* or *"I forgot."* It can show up sounding like this, *"I don't have the time to go to the bank"* or *"I forgot to call the bank to request my debit card for my Fun Debit card account."* It may seem meaningless, but I've seen it time and time again where this language allows for months to go by before accounts get open. You are no longer allowing these excuses to stop you. If you find yourself getting stuck, ask yourself, *Is it the language I'm using or are certain emotions like overwhelm or worry holding me back?* If "yes," use the tools from the previous category (Mindset) to move through what's stopping you.

On the **Accounts Actions Checklist**, you will see a clear list of the accounts (money homes) to have for your money. As you check off this list, it shows you what accounts you currently have and do not have, telling you what accounts to open so you can fill them up with your money. Since we are embracing a mindset of intentional living and conscious spending, each account has an intention. For your Bill Pay checking, the intention is to pay all your fixed monthly bills responsibly by paying them all out of this account and with gratitude. This creates peace of mind in knowing you have the correct amount of money in this account to cover paying all your important monthly bills. The intention for your Variable Debit Checking is conscious swiping on your debit card by having all your irregular expenses getting paid out of one account. This way, you're not overspending and eating into your savings money. The intention for the Fun Debit is having money designated for joy and play.

Tonia's Mini Money Message
Intentional living and conscious spending.

The intention for your Savings One account is that sweet financial security and peace of mind in knowing if a life situation comes your way, you have six months of reserves to pay for your "need" expenses. By putting money in this account, you are your own bank. The intention for your Retirement account is so that your financial future is secure. Putting money in this account creates financial peace of mind for your senior years. Your money is working for you. The intention for your Savings Two account is financial opportunity by putting money in here for items or experiences you want for yourself in the long term. This account allows for the mentality of "buy now, pay now" to come through so you no longer depend on your credit card to buy things. It's cash money baby, bye-bye to accumulating new debt!

The last account is Taxes. It's for those of you who do not have taxes taken out of your paycheck. The intention is being responsible for paying your taxes on time by putting the money in this account every time you get paid. This allows for you to be grateful for the income you receive and not dreading making more because you know you have the money sitting on the side come tax time.

After the checklist comes the section *Inspired Action Steps*. Here, you write down the steps to take to open the accounts you do not have. Allow the **Accounts Actions Checklist** to guide you in the actions to take to get it done! A lack of clarity will no longer be an excuse.

ACCOUNTS ACTIONS CHECKLIST

What to Do: Check off the accounts you currently have. If one of the accounts is not open, drop down to "Inspired Action Step" and write down, with empowering language, the actions to take to open the account.

I HAVE A...

☑ **Bill Pay Checking**
Intention: Pay all my fixed monthly bills responsibly and with gratitude.

☐ **Variable Debit Checking**
Intention: Conscious swiping on my irregular expenses so there's no overspending.

☐ **Fun Debit**
Intention: Having money designated for joy and play. Conscious swiping, no overspending or accumulating new debt.

☑ **Savings One**
Intention: Financial security and peace of mind. Do not spend. Remember, "I am my own bank."

☐ **Retirement**
Intention: My financial future is secure. Money is working for me.

☐ **Savings Two**
Intention: Financial opportunity. Long-term savings. "Buy now, pay now" mindset. No longer depending on my credit cards to buy things.

☐ **Taxes**
Intention: Being responsible for paying my taxes on time. Thank you for the income I receive.

INSPIRED ACTION STEPS:

What to Do:

List out the steps to take to open the accounts.

1) I will open two checking accounts with bank XYZ.

2) I will request two separate debit cards for each account.

*To download a blank version of the accounts actions checklist go to **www.toniag.com/rich-resources**

"Obstacles serve as an opportunity to call up our latent powers. They draw us out and make us strong."

– *Working With The Law*, Raymond Holliwell

This is your checklist for the accounts to have. When writing the *Inspired Action Steps*, please break down all the tasks to complete in order to open the bank account(s). For example, you intend to open a Fun Debit card account, but before you can open the account, you may first need to research a bank you want to use because you're not happy with your current one. This is step one on opening the new bank account. Step two is actually going to the bank and opening the account. Some steps may be that you want to close some bank accounts and that's perfectly okay. List out all the actions to take so you know what to do and have it written down all in one place. Remember to ask yourself as you are writing these actions out, are you using an empowering or disempowering language? Are you allowing your emotions to run the show versus decoding them? These are questions you ask continually, especially when you are resisting taking action or not taking action at all.

If you are worried about not having enough money to open these accounts, please let that story go. There are plenty of online banks that allow you to open accounts with just one dollar. Some great websites to do research on banks are nerdwallet.com and bankrates.com. They clearly show you what banks offer no fees and don't require minimum balances. What I love is they have all the information organized clearly for you, so it is easier to make a decision. Each one of you is different and are going to have different preferences for your banks; you get to choose which one feels best for you. Happy hunting for the accounts and banks that get you excited at what they are offering!

Once you have completed your **Accounts Action Checklist** and complete those actions (opening new accounts), you will follow through by filling out a new accounts worksheet, **Accounts Action Worksheet**, to clearly list all of your accounts and their singular purposes. See sample at right.

Joy Tip:

Make sure you have two separate debit cards for your Variable and Fun Debit card accounts. Write on your Fun Debit card "fun," and enjoy smiling every time you see fun written on your debit card.

ACCOUNTS ACTIONS WORKSHEET

What to Do: Fill in the below worksheet with your new accounts information.

Purpose of Account	Name	Acct #	Type	APY %	Min. Balance	Fee	Balance
Bill Pay	Bank xyz	0567	Checking	0%	$100	$15	$500
Variable Expenses Debit Card	Bank xyz	4601	Checking	0%	$100	$15	$300
Fun Debit Card	Bank xyz	6375	Checking	0%	$100	$15	$400
Savings One	Bank xyz	0310	Savings	.5%	$0	$0	$15000
Retirement	Bank xyz	0754	Roth IRA	9%	$0	$0	$10000
Sacvings Two	Bank xyz	0378	Savings	.5%	$0	$0	$6000
Taxes	Bank xyz	0395	Checking	0%	$0	$0	$3750

*To download a blank version of the accounts actions worksheet go to **www.toniag.com/rich-resources**

"Freedom is not living an obsessed, undisciplined life. Freedom is in being able to control your life and in making it what you want it to be."

– Raymond Holliwell

Celebration moment! Congratulations on taking action on your money magic blueprint! You are doing it. You are making the moves to improve your financial life. Take a moment. Pause. Breathe. Let that in. Celebrate the magnificent being you are. Now go and have some fun to enjoy yourself. Go and grab a favorite drink that you have at home and drink it somewhere beautiful. This doesn't necessarily involve you going anywhere to do this. It can be your favorite tea, coffee, soda, seltzer or wine and you can drink it looking out of your favorite window, or perhaps sitting outside.

FUN TIP: What drink will you have and where will you have it? I invite you to use your imagination and have fun with your creation.

Debt Action

This next stop on your money journey is a fun one, even though we are talking about debt. Here, we're taking action on paying off your debt and flipping the way you view it. You're claiming that shame by learning to love and appreciate your debt! I know we tend not to think of debt in this way, but it's powerful once we do. The intention is to thank debt for all it's given to you. I want you to recall all the experiences this debt brought your way. Really, close your eyes and think of some of these experiences in your mind. I'm sure it gave you some really nice things and experiences. Possibly a vacation, a gift to a loved one, education, self-care, maintenance for your car, a boiler for your house or some other household expense that came up unexpectedly. Call to mind the joy or relief it brought you in that moment. Feel it in your body.

Purchases with our credit card may be fun in the moment, but soon fades away once we get our statement balance. Debt robs us from the joy that purchase and/or experience brought us. This is because we have a "buy now, pay later" mindset and this is the mindset of the majority of our nation and our government. When we pay later, we feel the burden of that lump sum number and forget all the individual things we experienced from it. Using credit keeps us stuck in this mindset. Buy now, pay later is for instant gratification and being reactive to our wants. What we are exchanging is our joy and freedom to spend our income on the things we really value and desire! Take that in. What you are exchanging for this instant gratification is your JOY – sustainable JOY and freedom, and it's time to reclaim that.

This is why setting up the homes/accounts for your money is so important, because it creates the structure to support you in your spending habits so you no longer have to use a credit card. You will no longer be afraid to look at your credit balances. Instead, you'll be proud of what you're spending money on because you're doing it responsibly. You now have your Variable Expense and Fun Debit card to use instead of the credit card, so you are no longer adding to your current balance; making it easier to become debt-free and stay that way. You are changing your money spending habits and that's what creates sustainability.

Now, you focus on paying off the balances you have with the intention of joy and gratitude. The intention you set when you are spending the money is the energy behind the money you give. If you are not consciously setting an intention, your mind will do it for you, and most likely not a good one. What you give is what you attract back. When you spend with joy, you get joy back. When you spend with desperation, you get desperation back. While you are paying your debt, recall back what experiences this debt brought to you. The intention is to come from a place of appreciation, not desperation.

If you are someone who is already bringing joy and appreciation to your debt, great job and keep it up. In the **Debt Action Worksheet**, the graph portion is identical to the one in the previous stage. The difference is in this stage you now know the amount of *extra money* you can put towards your debt. Yes to that! Take the *extra money* you found on your **Savings Organization Worksheet** if you have a fixed income or your **Variable Income Organization Worksheet** if you have a variable income and place this amount into your **Debt Action Worksheet** in the *extra money* box. Additionally, there are three new sections: *Celebration, Joy Tips,* and *Inspired Action Steps* to remind you to stay in the space of gratitude with your debt and clear on the actions to take to pay off your debt. To show you what happens when you stay the course in paying off your debt below is an example of how your worksheet changes when you pay off the top debt and how your money rolls into your next debt helping you to pay it off quicker.

DEBT ACTION WORKSHEET

What to Do: From the **Debt Organization Worksheet,** fill in the below information for this worksheet.

For fixed income, get the *extra money* amount from the **Savings Organization Worksheet** (which we are using in the example below).

For variable income, get the *extra money* amount from the **Variable Income Organization Worksheet.**

Creditor	APR %	Due Date	Balance	Minimum Payment	+ Extra Money	= Amount to Pay	Current Payment Method
Discover	14.99%	20th	$1850	$41	$52	$93	Acct 0567
Macy's	25.99%	13th	$5000	$158	$	$158	Acct 0567
Visa	19.99%	16th	$3400	$90	$	$90	Acct 0567
Chase	14.99%	5th	$6500	$146	$	$146	Acct 0567
TOTAL			**$16750**	**$435**	**$52**	**$487**	

After you pay off your top debt (Discover), your updated worksheet will look like in the next table. Notice how the former *Amount To Pay* toward Discover is now carried over to *Extra Money* to pay towards your new top debt (Macy's).

*To download a blank version of the debt action worksheet go to **www.toniag.com/rich-resources**

Creditor	APR %	Due Date	Balance	Minimum Payment	+ Extra Money	= Amount to Pay	Current Payment Method
Macy's	25.99%	13th	$4750	$158	$93	$251	Acct 0567
Visa	19.99%	16th	$3250	$90	$	$90	Acct 0567
Chase	14.99%	5th	$6250	$146	$	$146	Acct 0567
TOTAL			**$14250**	**$394**	**$93**	**$487**	

After you pay off your top debt (Macy's), your updated worksheet will look like below. Notice how the former *Amount To Pay* toward Macy's is now carried over to *Extra Money* to pay towards your new top debt (Visa).

Creditor	APR %	Due Date	Balance	Minimum Payment	+ Extra Money	= Amount to Pay	Current Payment Method
Visa	19.99%	16th	$3250	$90	$251	$341	Acct 0567
Chase	14.99%	5th	$6250	$146	$	$146	Acct 0567
TOTAL			**$9500**	**$236**	**$251**	**$487**	

Celebration: Below, list out the debt you paid off to CELEBRATE all the work you put in!

- *Discover*

Joy Tip:
Gratitude – Money is a way to say thank you for your life's experiences. Connect to the experiences the above debt brought into your life and say thank you for it.

Thank you for …

- *The amazing vacation to Bahamas that I put on my Discover card.*

INSPIRED ACTION STEPS:

Below, write the actions to take for your debt to be in good standing. Please use this sheet to keep all your tasks for your debt actions in one place.

1) Write down due dates in my calendar.

———————————————

"Don't ask what the world needs.
Ask what makes you come alive, and go do it.
Because what the world needs is people who have come alive."

– Howard Thurman

———————————————

Great job in filling in the information! The cool aspect about this strategy is that as you pay off each debt, the amount of money getting paid to the next debt increases – thus your debt is getting paid off faster as you stick with making the payments. The trick is to take it one step at a time. Whenever you pay off a debt, the second one takes the first position. Paying off your debt is a marathon, not a sprint. The sweet spot is staying focused on paying off the top debt and adding in any extra money. While you pay the top debt down, you steadily pay the minimum balances for the rest of your debts.

Something I realized over the years doing this is when you become responsible and focused with your finances, money starts to come in from random different places! A client of mine when she finally decided to get clear on her debt and a plan to pay it down received an opportunity to make extra money after school, tutoring students. More extra money to pay down her debt. For me, I've had random money come to me in the form of a check from my PA house from my homeowner's insurance. This was years later and right when I needed that money! Keep the course and stay open for the opportunities.

Since you're putting in all this hard work, I've added a new section headed *Celebration!* Paying off debt is a cause for celebration. It's a place to list all the debts you paid off to remind yourself of how far you've come. It's a tribute to all your hard work. At times, you can be so intently focused on the debt-free future that along the way, you forget to look back at how far you've come and appreciate it. This is something you'll experience while being in the gap of where you want to go and being where you currently are. It's showing appreciation for all the steps completed that will allow it to feel pleasant and joyful. That's what the Celebration section is all about and why underneath it there's the *Joy Tips* section.

Under *Joy Tips*, you will write down all the joyful experiences that this debt has brought you. The trick is to allow this energy of joy to filter in when you're making payments, so you are coming from a place of gratitude versus resentment. The intention is to thank debt for all it's given to you, good or bad. It all served a purpose. You will hear that there is "good debt" and "bad debt." The best way to look at debt in terms of "good" and "bad" is asking yourself this question: "*Is this debt serving me or taking away from me?*" If it's taking away, let's get it paid off and not use that mode of payment again. The "good" and "bad" aspects are considerations when thinking about your credit history. What's important is to make your payments on time and to not max out your credit cards. Again, you are moving away from depending on using credit cards because you have a structure.

Lastly comes the section *Inspired Actions* for you to list any actions you choose to take with your debt to be in good standing and following the debt snowball method. Allow the thought of being debt-free to motivate you to stick with the plan you created, and allow the joy of what you did buy with the debt to flow in when you're making the payments to it (on time!).

Celebration moment! Congratulations on taking the actions to get yourself debt-free and into a healthy mindset in relation to your debt! Go you! You have the strategy, the motivation and the inspiration to get this done. I want you to go and have some fun to celebrate. I invite you to find a way to bring in fun without spending money. Use your imagination and creativity to find an activity you enjoy without money creating it for you.

> **FUN TIP:** Putting on my favorite playlist or song, whether I'm brushing my teeth, cooking, working or walking, is something that never fails to bring me joy. Why don't you give it a try, too? If you don't have a playlist, allow yourself to experiment with different music. Have fun exploring with music that makes you happy.

Expense Action

We are rolling along and continuing with setting the intention of giving from joy and gratitude in our everyday spending of our expenses. We want to anchor into giving from a place of high vibes and acting from the emotions that are in alignment with this high vibration. What we give, we attract back. In this category, the purpose is to be clear on the actions to take in paying your bills on time and from the correct payment account.

Your **Fixed Expense Actions Worksheet** allows you to have all your information in one place for paying your bills. One worksheet to rule them all. This way, when it's time to pay a bill, you are not getting stuck in "what to do." This worksheet tells you what bill to pay, the amount, when to pay it, from which account and a nifty check off box to keep track of what's been paid or not. It's all about clear direction for your actions.

The *Joy Tips* section of this worksheet reminds you to take the time out to say thank you when paying your bills. I invite you to practice saying thank you to every bill you pay. When you do, paying your bills becomes a magical experience of gratitude. Imagine, every time you pay your phone bill you have the opportunity to say, *"Thank you, phone company, for allowing me to communicate with my loved ones."* When you pay with gratitude, money will return back to you with gratitude. Money loves to play like that. You are laying down the healthy money habits for paying your bills. Here is your **Fixed Expense Actions Worksheet** to guide you in knowing exactly when your bills are due.

FIXED EXPENSE ACTIONS WORKSHEET

FIXED EXPENSES	AMOUNT	DUE DATE	NEW PAYMENT METHOD	BILL PAID (check box)
Mortgage/Rent	$1800	1st	Bill Pay Checking	X
Cell Phone	$100	5th	Bill Pay Checking	X
Chase	$146	5th	Bill Pay Checking	X
Car Insurance	$100	7th	Bill Pay Checking	X
Electric	$100	10th	Bill Pay Checking	
Macy's	$158	13th	Bill Pay Checking	
Gym Membership	$75	16th	Bill Pay Checking	
Visa	$90	16th	Bill Pay Checking	
Spotify	$10	17th	Bill Pay Checking	
Apple storage	$10	18th	Bill Pay Checking	
Gas	$100	19th	Bill Pay Checking	
Discover	$93	20th	Bill Pay Checking	
Internet	$80	21st	Bill Pay Checking	
Hulu	$5	21st	Bill Pay Checking	
Car Payment	$250	25th	Bill Pay Checking	
Netflix	$10	28th	Bill Pay Checking	
Cable TV	$120	30th	Bill Pay Checking	

*To download a blank version of the fixed expense actions worksheet go to **www.toniag.com/rich-resources**

What to Do: Fill in the worksheet with the following information:

- List all of your expenses that have due dates (from your **Expense Information Worksheet**)
- List the *New Payment Method* account (from your **Accounts Action Worksheet**)
- List each debt's *Amount To Pay* (from your **Debt Actions Worksheet**) as debts are fixed expenses.
- List out each subscription as subscriptions are fixed expenses.
- *List all expenses in order of due date.*

Joy Tip:

Gratitude – Money is a way to say thank you for your life's experiences. Connect to the services and things you receive from the above payments and say thank you for it.

Example:
"Thank you for the roof over my head," when paying rent.
"Thank you for allowing me to communicate with my loved ones," when paying phone bill.

INSPIRED ACTION STEPS:

Below, write the actions to take for your expenses. Please use this sheet to keep all your tasks for this in one place.

1) Go online and make payment for Discover card.
2) Call credit card to dispute charges on my card.
3) Call cell phone company to ask why my bill was more money this month.
4) Switch my gym membership from my credit card to my bill pay account.

"Argue for your limitations and you get to keep them."

– Elizabeth Gilbert, *Big Magic*

You are incredible and getting so good at developing your organizational skills! By having your due dates listed in one place, you are no longer giving your money away to late fees and non-sufficient fund (NSF) fees to banks and credit card companies. This is why you put all your information in one place. It may feel like a lot of copying and pasting from one stage to the next – it is, and it's all to build your money system. The Freedom stage (this stage!) is the final resting place for your numbers. So celebrate this is the last time you will be copying and pasting them over. You got this.

Here's a tip I learned from working with my clients if you have automatic payments set up for your bills. Sometimes automatic payments are set up to be responsible in paying your bills on time, just in case you forget when it's due. But, what can also happen is forgetting when the debit comes out of your account. Before you know it, you look at your account and you get hit with a NSF fee because there's not enough money in there to cover it. Hell no to that!! You now have way too many money homes to put your money in to let this continue happening. These fees are not cheap and could be going to your savings, fun, Bill Pay or debt accounts. No more flushing your money down the toilet in fees. Hence why this worksheet is so important.

Your **Fixed Expense Actions Worksheet** prevents this from happening by keeping all of your due dates in one place. You can put this into action now by printing out this worksheet and hanging it somewhere you will see it to remind you when your bills are due. If you prefer a digital option, enter the due dates into a Google calendar (or whichever type you use). The great thing with doing this digitally is that you can set it up to repeat every month, on the same day, so each month you know when your bills are due. You enter it once and never have to do it again. Lovely.

Congratulations on reclaiming your money power in paying your bills! Celebrate that you are moving into intentional living and no longer giving your money away to things wastefully. *Intentional living, conscious spending* is the mindset you are taking on in your spending and in life as a whole. Now let's have some fun to celebrate.

> **FUN TIP:** One of my favorite songs I love to dance to is "Dance Bailalo" by Kat DeLuna. I invite you to put on your favorite song and dance!

Tonia's Mini Money Life Lessons

The Hijack

I'm lying in bed, first waking up. I open my eyes and I'm attacked by my thoughts. An all-out assault on my brain….

"You haven't visited your nephews.

Seven years in business and this is where you're at.

You're not eating right.

You're not taking care of your body.

What are you doing with yourself?

You haven't visited your friends, you're such a bad friend.

You haven't posted on social media.

You need to go through your emails.

You watch way too much TV.

How are you going to find a partner if you never go out or go on dates?

You're not making enough money.

You need to work out."

What the fuck! I just woke up. How in the world am I waking up this way? Yesterday was an amazing, great day. Okay, let me calm down and do my Reiki. Hands on my crown, my third eye (it's still not stopping), back of my head. I get to my solar plexus and just stop. Okay, let me go journal and see if I can write this out of me or uncover what's going on. First, I go to my altar, say my affirmations, use my Wisdom of the Earth essences (my personal assistants and secret weapon) and then go and journal. I do my three pages of mindless writing like the brilliant Julia Cameron suggests and move along my day. I am fucking off. I hate the world, I do not want to be bothered by people. I'm just in a negative, dark, scarcity mindset and I cannot seem to get myself out of it. I sage, meditate, pull cards, light candles, phone a friend, dance it out and still nada, go for a walk and nothing.

Basically, to sum it up into one soundbite, my way of being and mindset is "I don't care." Everyone I come into contact with annoys me. There's no reason for me to feel this way. Nothing triggered me or happened. I woke up like this and not in an empowering way, like Beyonce puts it. It's just shitty. With all the work I've done and awareness I have, I thought I was past days like this and feeling like this. For fuck's sake, I'm an abundance coach and my essence is joy. The reason I do all I do is because of joy. What the hell?! Why am I broken? Why does this still happen? What am I doing wrong? How can I fix this? When am I going to feel normal again?

Again, an all-out attack on everything I haven't accomplished yet: "Yeah right, who are you to write a book? Look at you, you're a mess. Keep dreaming in thinking you'll ever have your own TV show and podcast. You'll never have a five-figure month *without being stressed out and killing yourself. Who are you to call yourself a money expert? Even if you finish the book, no one is going to read it. If you do make it, you'll fail under the pressure of fame. People are going to ridicule you. Your friends are going to think you're nuts. Your family is going to think you're nuts. If you were you ten years ago, you would hate who you were right now. Visualize your life, my ass. That's a bunch of bullshit. You're never going to have it."*

Sweet baby Jesus, this chatter is ruthless today. I think I'm just going to stay home and watch television to shut this mind of mine off. As I do, I have a knot in my stomach because I know I'm avoiding my life, but I don't care because I do not have the energy to do any more to stop it. The best I can do is numb it and at least I'm not doing it with food or alcohol. Television is the poison for today. I know as soon as I fall asleep, it will finally stop. I put myself to bed. Please go away. Morning comes, I open my eyes and nothing.

The only way I can explain it is that my mind got hijacked by my ego. On some days it happens and there's nothing I can do about it, and it helps for me to identify it. It's a mind hijack. Saying that allows acceptance to come through versus judgment. This makes all the world of difference. It allows me to laugh at what's happening, a surrender, if you will. On days you find your mind not cooperating with your abundant mindset, just say to yourself, *"I'm being hijacked."* Witness what is going on by putting yourself in the third person. Trust me, you'll get a very entertaining show. Enjoy!

Income Action

Okay, the next stop on this money journey is income! It is your right to enjoy the money you earn. Your income is the money hub and the most important step to address with your money. Not transferring it to the correct accounts each month means your money will continue getting lost. When you are feeling unmotivated to put these structures in place, bear in mind that the purpose of the structures is to make sure your money goes towards the things you want, intentionally. You are worth paying yourself for the money you earn by putting it into your savings, and without the transfers getting done, you will overspend. You deserve to keep your income, so embrace knowing where it all goes. This way, money can work for you instead of you working for your money.

Your **Fixed or Variable Income Actions Worksheet** is the map for you to see clearly the transfers to make with your income and a way for you to keep track of when you've completed them. It's accountability and clarity on the actions to take to form your new healthy money habits with your income. You already did the heavy lifting in the first two stages of figuring out what the numbers are. Here we are laying them out in a clear format, so all your income transfers live in one place. The intention of this worksheet is to be clear on the actions to take: knowing the amount of income you have coming in (calculated in the Focus stage), knowing the amount to transfer into the designated home/account (calculated in the Foundation stage), and keeping track of when you completed the transfer (this stage, Freedom).

For those of you with a fixed income, you are using the **Fixed Income Actions Worksheet.** Once this worksheet is filled out, you know exactly where to put your paychecks once they come in. You will see that there are additional rows for Retirement and Savings Two. In the next category, *Savings Action*, you will learn the milestones to reach for your savings – breaking your savings amounts into different accounts (Retirement and Savings Two) so you have balance in your savings money homes.

The second worksheet is **Variable Income Actions**. You are taking the numbers you calculated from your **Variable Income Organization Worksheet** and putting it in a clear format so you know exactly how to split your deposits as they come in.

Joy Tips:

Clarity on what actions to take with your income and transferring the money to their designated money homes in turn creates freedom with your money.

As you make each transfer, sprinkle some gratitude on top of it, say thank you for the money you have no matter what the amount!

FIXED INCOME ACTIONS WORKSHEET

What to Do: Fill in the below worksheet using information from your **Fixed Income Organization Worksheet** and **Savings Organization Scenarios.**

GROUP NAMES	AMOUNT	ACCOUNT	COMPLETED
Fixed Expenses	$3260	Bill Pay Checking - 0567	
Extra money to debt	$52	Bill Pay Checking - 0567	
Buffer money to fixed expenses	$52	Bill Pay Checking - 0567	
Variable Expenses	$620	Variable Debit Checking - 4601	
Fun Expenses	$985	Fun Debit - 6375	
Savings One	$156	Savings One - 0310	
Retirement	-	Retirement - 0754	
Savings Two	-	Savings Two - 0378	

*To download a blank version of the fixed income actions worksheet go to **www.toniag.com/rich-resources**

"Every day my income increases
whether I am working, playing, or sleeping."

- *Money Is My Friend*, Phil Laut

As you enter the numbers from previous worksheets, the roadmap for your monthly income appears! It's nicely organized all in one place for you to see. For those who have a fixed income, remember these transfers are broken out by the income you make in a month. I suggest making these transfers every time you receive a paycheck. If you get paid bi-monthly, you split the amount for that transfer into two. If you get paid weekly, you split the transfer into four. At the end of the month, you check off that whole transfer amount as completed.

For those who have a variable income, you split out your income every time you receive a deposit (you can total up your deposits for the day or end of the week). I suggest not allowing yourself to go any longer than a week. You keep re-using this chart for those deposits. For those who are Excel savvy, you can create this into a worksheet. Whether your income is fixed or variable each transfer will get sprinkled with some gratitude. We say thank you to money no matter what the amount! Congratulations on having a clear path for your money (income) to go to its home (bank accounts)!

The next worksheet, **Balance Sheet** is a bonus tool to support you in knowing the flow of your money depending on the dates the money comes in and goes out. Back in the day, when writing checks was a common practice, you would receive a balance book along with your checks. In the digital age, balancing a checkbook has become a lost art.

The balance book helps you figure out the timing of it all so you can adjust what's not working by knowing the balance remaining as you pay out each expense. Your monthly income may cover the full amount of your expenses, but it's the timing of paying out those expenses that do not jive with when the income comes in.

For example, at the beginning of the month you may find your whole paycheck goes quickly because big expenses go out, like your rent or mortgage. This means that until your next paycheck, your cashflow is tight. If you have credit cards or other bills that are due at the beginning of the month, you can call the relevant companies up and ask if they can switch your due date for the time in the month when you receive your second paycheck. This is the power of the balance sheet.

Here is the traditional layout of a balance sheet. These are the main components to it: date, purpose, payment amount, deposit amount and balance. The date you enter is the day you make the payment or receive the deposit. You put the dates in sequential order (as a reminder, this information is listed on your **Fixed Expense Actions Worksheet**). In the *purpose* column, you put who you are making the payment to – for example, it might be rent or to pay for your cable. The column for *payment amount* is for all items that are expenses and are going out of the account. The column for *deposit amount* is for all items that are income and coming into the account. The *balance remaining* is the number you get by taking the previous balance's number (when you first start, it will be the current amount in your checking account) and either subtracting or adding it depending on if it is an expense or a deposit. This number goes in the *balance* column and you repeat for each line. Take a look at the balance sheet to see if this is something you'll like to experiment with and if it will support you in keeping track of your numbers.

"Clarity creates power."

- Tony Robbins

BALANCE SHEET

Account: Bill Pay - 0567

DATE	PURPOSE	PAYMENT AMOUNT ($ OUT)	DEPOSIT AMOUNT ($ IN)	BALANCE ($ REMAINING)
		-	+	Current balance checking account: $500
10/1	Paycheck		$2562.50	$3062.50
10/1	Rent	$1800		$1262.50
10/1	Transfer to Variable Debit Checking - 4601 (half of transfer amount)	$310		$952.50
10/2	Transfer to Fun Debit - 6375	$492.50		$460
10/2	Transfer to Savings One - 0310	$78		$382
10/5	Cell Phone	$100		$282
10/5	Chase	$146		$136
10/13	Macy's	$158		$-22
	Call credit card to change due date to later in the month			
10/15	Paycheck		$2562.50	$2540.50
10/16	Transfer to Variable Debit - 4601	$310		$2230.50
10/16	Transfer to Fun Debit - 6375	$492.50		$1738
10/16	Transfer to Savings One - 0310	$78		$1660
10/16	Gym	$75		$1585
10/16	Visa	$90		$1495

*To download a blank version of the balance sheet go to
www.toniag.com/rich-resources

The convenience in mapping out the monthly transactions for your Bill Pay account, is to know exactly how much money you have remaining at the end of the month and through out the month. Now that you have your **Fixed Expense Actions Worksheet** with all your due dates on it, you can easily fill in the balance sheet to see what is going out. For some, you may be freaking out right now because this is too confusing, detailed and meticulous. You're not a bookkeeper and I understand that. Let's find the method that best fits for you to get the same result, which is knowing the amount of money remaining after the money comes in and goes out.

Method One: If you are a person who loves spreadsheets like I do, you can enter the details into a spreadsheet and let the spreadsheet do the math for you.

Method Two: You can take the balance sheet format and do it with a good old-fashioned pen and paper. On a piece of paper, write *date, description, money in, money out and balance* and fill it in.

Method Three: Don't create a balance sheet, and instead, use a calculator. Take the amount of your paycheck and subtract all the expenses due until the money goes to zero. Check the date of that expense and see if more money will come in by that point.

Mapping the money coming in and going out for the month takes away the worried feeling of *"do I have enough, or will my account go negative?"* This is also why we have a group for your money called *buffer amount to fixed expenses*, so this doesn't happen. When there is enough money in your savings, you can buffer your Bill Pay account with one months' worth of expenses so that you do not have to worry about going negative. If money is tight, this is a great tool to use and a good way to keep yourself accountable on where your money is going.

It's not necessary to do this for your debit card accounts. That was the whole point of creating different spending accounts (debit and fun) to figure out how much to put in each one so that you are responsible in your swiping and can enjoy doing it guilt-free! If you're unsure of how much money is in your debit card accounts you can go online and look at the balances before you swipe. We have the Bill Pay account as the focus because that's where the big bills get paid out of and if you're late on a payment, it can affect your credit score –you're also dealing with those late fees and NSF fees. No thank you to that, we would rather have that money going to savings or fun. Conscious spending is at work here.

Celebrate yourself for all the work you have done so far. You are worth celebrating! Congratulations on making the money you earn work for you, instead of the other way round! Go and do something fun to celebrate. I invite you to use your imagination and find something that makes you happy that doesn't involve spending money. Let's embrace finding the simple joys in life.

> **FUN TIP:** Go outside on an exploration to discover what things around you ignite the spark of joy within. If you can't go outside, you can do the same indoors. When you do this, you may see things that were always there but that you've never really noticed before – for example, you may realize a pot plant or a picture hanging on the wall brings you joy. Let your eyes lead the way.

Savings Action

Savings is the road to enjoying your money. An important and great affirmation from Phil Laut that describes how to do this is, *"A part of all I earn is mine to keep."* A part of what you earn is yours to keep and this happens through nurturing the habit of savings.

You create financial peace of mind when you begin to pay yourself first through your savings. In the last stage, you figured out what this "pay yourself" savings number is.

In this category, you'll build on that and learn the milestones to hit in order to break out your money into different savings accounts, creating balance with your savings money. These milestones give you the actions to take and are what create the healthy new habits for your savings. It's your personal money bank that provides financial freedom and more control of your life. Let's review the **Savings Actions Worksheet** to guide you along the road to homing your savings and learning a strategy to split them between your Savings One, Retirement and Savings Two.

Joy Tip:
Congratulations! With this sheet, you created balance in your financial life, and you did this when you started with Milestone #1! Enjoy the financial peace of mind and freedom.

*To download a blank version of the savings actions worksheet go to **www.toniag.com/rich-resources**

SAVINGS ACTIONS WORKSHEET

Goal - *Create 3 months of Needs expenses
in a savings account and save for retiremement!*

What to Do: Check off the below milestones as you achieve them.

☑ **Milestone #1:** Yes, I have a savings account!

☑ **Milestone #2:** Yes, I have $500 saved

☑ **Milestone #3:** Yes, I have $1,000 saved.

☑ **Milestone #4:** Yes, I have one month of *Needs Expenses* saved. Celebration time!!

☐ **Milestone #5:** Yes, I have three months of *Needs Expenses* saved in Savings One.

☐ ***Milestone ACTION:*** After achieving Milestone 5, start splitting your monthly savings amount. Half goes into Saving One and the other half into Retirement.

☐ **Milestone #6:** Yes, I have six months of *Needs Expenses* saved in Savings One. Celebration time!!

☐ ***Milestone ACTION:*** After achieving Milestone 6, open your Savings Two account. Continue splitting your monthly savings amount two ways. Now half goes into Retirement and the other half into Savings Two.

Congratulations on investing in your future!!

Note: The intention of Savings One is to always have 6 months of your Needs expenses saved. If your Needs Expenses increase, save accordingly to keep 6 months of Needs expenses in Savings One.

Okay, let's go into a little more detail about the different milestones listed on the worksheet.

Milestone 1: To have a savings account open and available to put money into. If you don't, go and open one, now. Yes, really – right now. Ally Bank allows you to open a savings account without even going to the bank. I'm just saying, what's stopping you? You don't have the money? Oh, you can open it with just one dollar. You don't have the time? It takes fifteen minutes and you can do it from your home. Breaking the old habits and leaving the old stories behind starts by taking action on the new, so open that bank account.

Milestones 2 and 3: You are reaching certain dollar amounts in your Savings One account. When you have $1,000 in savings, celebrate yourself. Recognize you shifted yourself out of the 69% of Americans who have less than $1,000 saved and into the 31% who have more than that saved. My mission is to get as many people as I can out of the 69% and into the 31%. Financial security for all. Keep it up and remember the intention is to not have this account go below $1,000. Fix in your mind: *"This account creates my financial security and peace of mind."* It's not the *"I really want that shirt or thing"* account. In the financial world, they call this the "emergency savings" account. We learned about disempowering language;

therefore, we are not setting for our savings the intention of emergency. Heck no.

We refer to this account as Savings One. You get to choose what fun name you want to associate this account with. Something that feels good and is inspiring to you. A good indication is if you smile every time you read the name or laugh. I call mine my "security" savings account. If the crap hits the fan, which at times in life it does, I'm calm and stress-free because I have money saved in the bank of Tonia (my savings). You want to continue increasing the amount of money in this account, thereby increasing your security and increasing your own personal bank. Just imagine, the bank of:_____ (insert your name here). Allow that feeling of being your own bank flood over your body.

Tonia's Mini Money Message
Allow that feeling of being your own bank
flood over your body.

In Milestone 4 and 5, I mention your *need expenses* number. This is the number we figured out with your expenses in stage one, on your **Expense Information Worksheet**. This is another reason why it's good to have your expenses in groups, so you know the milestone number to hit with your savings. Everything serves a larger purpose. You want a minimum of three months of reserves in Savings One, in the event you lose your job or couldn't work for any reason. That way, you can still provide for you or your family for at least three months. This takes you out of the financial survival mindset and being a slave to your job by living paycheck to paycheck. It's time to thrive, not just survive. Suffering is optional and on this road trip we're moving from lack to abundance. Here, the amount you save gets split and put into two accounts: Savings One and Retirement. At this milestone, it's time to start investing in your future financial security by opening a retirement account, if you don't already have one.

In *Milestone 6*, you have six months of *need expenses* in Savings One and once you do, stop saving in this account. You have your peace of mind knowing that if crap hits the fan, you are financially okay for six months. Now, the money you were putting into Savings One will go into another savings account where you can spend the money too! This is the way you no longer accumulate debt. When you want to buy something, the money is there for you to use. It's the habit of saving in this account that has you no longer creating new debt or relying on a credit card to buy things, along with using the Variable and Fun Debit cards. The intention is to create balance by having multiple savings accounts. Just for fun, what will you call your Savings Two account? I call mine my "money opportunities" account. What will you call yours?

You now have your savings roadmap and the milestones to hit when it comes to your savings. You are paying yourself for your current financial security with Savings One, for your future security with your Retirement account, and for fun long-term spending with Savings Two. Remember, if your expenses happen to increase, make sure you add to your Savings One to match that increase. Revel in seeing these accounts grow. Savor the freedom and peace of being responsible with your money and relish that money is working for you!

Hooray to you for completing the Freedom stage! Congratulations, you're a warrior. You now have a strategy and a clear list of actions to take for your money categories.

Celebrate knowing the pathway to manage your money and use it as the tool it is. As the negative chatter comes up, love up on it! Do not shame it, judge it, or hate it! It is a part of you. Hating on it only feeds into the belief of incompleteness. Your negative chatter or shadow side is a part of you, whether you like it or not, so you might as well get familiar with it. If you are courageous enough to listen to it with a loving, non-judgmental ear, most of the time, it has a lot of wisdom to share. It's what gives you the power to reclaim parts of yourself that have been ruled by fear. I invite you to welcome it and look at it as an invitation to reclaim a part of yourself. You are now moving along the road to the Flow stage, where you will learn the tools to face that fear, to create sustainable change in your life by mastering the greatest tool of all, YOU.

> **FUN TIP:** I invite you to take a dollar bill out and write on it, "I am my own economic system," and keep this in your wallet to remember the truth, that you are the master of money. For double fun, write the same thing on another dollar bill and go and spend this dollar bill. Put this in circulation and gift this message to a complete stranger. What a beautiful message to give.

Chapter 16:
Stage Four - Flow

Congratulations on creating the clarity, structure and healthy new habits for your money system by soaring through the Focus, Foundation, and Freedom stages! Welcome to the fourth stage in your money journey: Flow! Here, you stop being a victim to money, to yourself, and to any external circumstances. When you allow external circumstances and things to influence your internal space, you live in the world of illusions. One of them being that the money plan creates lasting peace of mind, freedom, security or independence. I discovered, not to my liking at all, the grand joke once having the perfect money system is that it does not create true peace of mind, freedom, security or independence. Rather, any such feelings you have are temporary, and that's part of the illusion of money.

Money doesn't create anything. Money is a tool. The definition of a "tool" according to dictionary.com is *"a device or implement, especially one held in the hand, used to carry out a particular function."* Money supports you in carrying out a particular function and without your hand, it cannot function. Money has no power! Money is neutral. You hold the power by creating the intention behind the function of it. If you are not doing it consciously, then your subconscious is doing it for you. It's time to awaken to the power within you and see the unlimited supply of life's gifts available to you now. When you make this connection with yourself, something happens. You feel a connection to something bigger, to a oneness in the world. The common thread is that it's something bigger than yourself, and yet it connects you to your oneness and your wholeness. The way you experience this connection is unique to each individual.

For me, I felt connected to this "one" energy and to nature. I remember the moment it happened. I was visiting my soul sister Melissa, who lived in Portland, Oregon at the time. We decided to go on a trip to Breitenbush Hot Springs. No Wi-Fi, no cell service. It was an unplug from technology and a plug into nature. We decided to get up at dawn the next morning to go into the all-female hot spring. As we walked over, we saw it was empty and that we had it all to ourselves – what a gift! While sitting in the hot spring, there was this serene, magical fog surrounding us. A mystery among the beauty. As the sun began to come up, the fog started to disappear in the rays of the sun and it unveiled this majestic canvas of trees. It was breathtaking. It was a moment I would never forget because I felt more alive than ever before and I received that gift of presence.

I continued to lay there in the spring, allowing nature to hold my back with her stones and feeling her warmth all around me with her blanket of hot water. I started to put my hands on my body and do my morning self-Reiki practice, chakra by chakra. As I did, I heard her speak to me. Nature. Mother. I felt held and connected to something so much bigger. I lost myself in the vastness of it all to show me I'm connected to it ALL. It affected me, it changed me and how I view nature. She is the Source. This Source is an untapped well of energy, inspiration, power, love and courage that's available to all of us and exists within all of us.

This is what the Flow stage is all about: connecting you to these self-truths, knowing you are a magnificent being just by being yourself. When you align with this truth, you can be an expression of love and do your best in all you do. When you operate from this place, money is a natural byproduct of what you receive back. You are not working for money. You work because you choose to, it's an expression of your greatness, so sustaining healthy money habits is a pleasure. Maintaining your money is an act of self-love. You are taking responsibility for your life and wellbeing. We are using our mind, body, and soul to lead us to our most authentic selves and become our own money gurus. It's best to remember it's a marathon, not a sprint. Slow and steady wins the sustainability race.

For now, I want to support you in sustaining the money habits and system you created in the first three stages because even though the money system does not create lasting peace of mind, it does cover having peace of mind over your finances by managing it as the great tool it is. Money does touch every aspect of our life so we want mastery over this tool and the convenience it offers. That's why we are learning to use money dates to keep us accountable to managing our money. Then in the chapters to follow, we learn the tools to connect to your mind, body and soul to sustain abundance in your internal life, so you are not constantly tuned in to the scarcity and lack that the outside world embraces.

Money Myths & Illusions

There are many money myths that are incorrect and therefore make people view money through a lens of scarcity and lack. Two popular ones being: *"Money doesn't grow on trees"* and *"Money is the root of all evil."* How many times have we heard these? As we learned in Stage One, the stories we tell ourselves and the beliefs we have influence our reality and what we attract! Yes, money does not grow on trees and money is not so limited as the saying implies. There is more than enough to go around, many times around. The problem is the unequal distribution of money to a small percentage instead of the whole. There's enough. Therefore, we will anchor our thoughts to an abundant mindset knowing *there's enough* and channel our mind to get the enough we desire.

Let's discuss the next popular one that I adore, *"Money is the root of all evil."* What a perfect saying to keep us stuck in our unhappy financial situations and scared to take action to earn more because it will turn us evil – or better yet, not enjoying what we have because it's somehow sinful. To break the myth down further, money is neither good nor evil. When handling money, a person is using it with either good or bad intentions. Money has nothing to do with it. That's why we embrace the mantra *intentional living and conscious spending.* We are intentional with our thoughts that influence our actions and conscious of our spending!

Here is a money myth truth bomb that will most likely burn your eyes when you read it. The truth is, money is not the reason you don't have what you want – you are or rather, your thinking is. So, let's start here: stop blaming money for not having the life you want. It's not money's fault, it's your thinking. Trust me, this one really hurt when I realized it's not money standing in my way, it's me. That's what the Flow stage is all about, learning to get out of your own way, so the FLOW of life can support you. Change your thinking, change your life! If you say money is the root of all evil, it will be, and you will be missing out on all the good money can do in the world versus focusing on all the evil it can do. Let's check off the unsubscribe box in your mind to *"Money does not grow on trees,"* and that *"Money is the root of all evil."* Now, let's throw these beliefs out in your mind's trash bin, just like you do with spam mail that's clogging up your inbox. Throw that mental trash out! Remember to keep emptying your mind's money trash bin on this journey; it fills up quickly with false truths.

> ### Tonia's Mini Money Message
> Keep emptying your mind's money trash bin.

You are learning to BE, and allow your "beingness" to drive your "doingness" so you're not blocking yourself from your greatness. Don't buy into the myth that greatness is picky or designated for some and not for you. Unsubscribe to that thinking and subscribe to it being for everyone, because it is! The intention is to move out of the prison of illusions that are grounded in scarcity, lack, fear, doubt and worry, and lean into the light of truths that are grounded in abundance, love, beauty and wonder. The simple truth is when we act from a place rooted in scarcity, all we see in our lives and in the world is what is missing. When we act from a place rooted in abundance, all we see in our lives and in the world is all that exists. Scarcity roots us in lack and abundance roots us in knowing that there's enough. It's time to dispel these illusions so we can see in our lives that we are enough, and that all around us there is enough.

First, let's step into a world of what life is like when we act from abundance.

Wonder. Connection. Laughter. Kindness. Celebration. Sharing your light, love and peace is what's available through abundance. Awakening to the possibility of a new way of being that is Joy and Peace. Intentional living. Being aware of all the beauty in the world. Seeing how beautiful it is, how beautiful she is. Treating Mother Nature with the love and respect she deserves. Treating *yourself* with the love and respect you deserve. To demand it because it's possible and is available to you right here and right now. For you and everyone around you to have hearts full of peace. To know you are safe, held, worthy, loved, honored and cherished. To mother and father yourself and your inner child, the way you wanted to be parented when you were younger – becoming the ideal parents to your inner child.

There is so much love and abundance all around us that we walk by every day. Air, water, love, connection, touch, sunrise, sunsets … and it is all free. Yet we allow ourselves to pass these gifts by every single day. Saying "no" to the joy and abundance of the world. All it takes is a moment's pause to receive it and take it in. All it takes is stopping. Getting present in the moment. We do this by feeling the sun on our faces, feeding our bodies the vitamin D it needs. Recognizing the rain falling from the sky, giving us the water our bodies need. Noticing the beautiful relationship we have with the trees. They take the carbon dioxide our bodies don't need and return it back with the air we breathe. Giving and receiving in its most organic form. So beautiful. Stay still, hear and feel the beating of your heart. It's so strong. So capable. So brave. So giving. This is available to us at all times. In every moment we exist.

How are we not sitting around in awe of the beauty all around us? Captivated by the abundance of the present moment. Allowing ourselves to feel this energy and letting it fill us up. Presence. Awareness. It is time for us to claim these gifts and release the illusion of the false world of material things. The illusion of happiness existing outside of us. The illusion of doing more to achieve more. The illusion that money is power and happiness. Release these illusions. Tap into all that exists within you. All our bodies need are food, water, air and love. That is all we need to live. Please stop confusing needs with wants. Anything outside of these four things is a want. Our needs all exist for free. Yes, if we plant our own food it can be for free. So, what are we chasing? What story is in the background and running the show? What illusions are we living in?

Please wake up from these illusions and see the abundance that surrounds you. You don't have to do anything to be worthy. If you are breathing, you are worthy. It's that simple. Your breath doesn't judge. Joy exists in the simplicity of life and the simplicity of life exists in The Now. In this moment, you have all that you need and want. Please get present to it. Be grateful for it. Your purpose is to awaken to this truth and to be the expression of your greatness, your authenticity and your joy, and to share that expression in the world. You are special and unique. Capable of remarkable, beautiful things. We are individual pieces to one beautiful puzzle. We are one and connected to this one source. No one is alone and we are all here to serve a purpose. So wake up to your calling, wake up to your gifts, wake up to the abundance that exists all around you right now. Free yourself by freeing your mind.

This is what's possible in being rooted in the true essence of abundance and what you are being robbed off by living through the lens of scarcity and lack. Let's explore scarcity (abundance's kryptonite) to know what to look out for in order for us to have rich lives, outside just the riches of money. Here is a quote from Lynne Twist that sums it up best. "It would be easy to assume that all this talk about appreciation and sufficiency is really aimed at those who have so little that they must learn to appreciate what little they have or sink in despair. It is just as true of people with great wealth and surplus. They can, and often do, become lost in the sea of excess, flooded with things, houses, cars, and stuff, such that they lose any sense of an inner life or meaning beyond the money. Mother Teresa once noted what she called 'the deep poverty of the soul' that afflicts the wealthy and had said that the poverty of the soul in America was deeper than any poverty she had seen anywhere on earth."

Scarcity is the toxin corrupting our world today and the mindset that rules the majority of people. Scarcity has us acting from a place of desperation and through this lens all we see is what doesn't exist. It reinforces all the lack surrounding us. It blinds us to what already exists in our lives and has us complaining about all we do not have. The conversations sound like this:

"I'll be happy when …"
"When I have this _____ then I can _____"
"Once I make this amount of $ I can do _____"
"This raise …"

"This relationship …"
"This job …"

By focusing on what's outside of us we are allowing outwardly things to show us our worth, as opposed to what's inside of us. This makes happiness always a future destination and never a place we experience here and now. It keeps us in an endless chase for these false illusions and truths. The word "abundance" has become very trendy and used to manipulate for the sake of marketing and selling things.

An illusion to dispel is that "abundance" is reaching the point that you have more than you need and then are wasteful because you are so abundant you can throw things out without caring. That's not abundant, that's mindless and being wasteful. According to Dictionary.com, the definition of abundance is *"an extremely plentiful or over sufficient quantity or supply, overflowing fullness, affluence; wealth."* Meaning you TRUST that there is more than enough for all: a plentiful, sufficient, and overflowing supply for all. Right now, scarcity has us taking this overflow and hoarding it for ourselves for a false sense of security. This doesn't just have to do with money (I.E. the toilet paper shortage during the covid 19 pandemic is the perfect example of this). Later on in this stage, we will talk about trust and overflow.

For now, if you really want to know the essence of abundance, go outside in nature. That's abundance, she's abundance and right now we are destroying her because of this need for more. We are killing our rainforests and our supply of oxygen to make more space for commerce, and for what? More clothes, food, electronics, furniture, and things? Meanwhile, we have more than enough – so much so that we are wasting an average of 35% of our food supply in the United States, according to an article in the *NY Times*. 35% being wasted, not going to the ones in need. The hard truth is that the people who are poor are not getting any of this "abundance" of stuff. In fact, they are the ones doing the labor for all of it to happen and are underpaid in doing it. Yet, advertising and marketing is a billion-dollar industry aimed at brainwashing us into believing their product is what we need to feel happy and successful. When does this accumulation of more ever end?

This scarcity mindset allows us to justify raping our planet of all of its natural resources. See through that illusion. We are willing to sacrifice our planet because we want more of the latest fashion at faster speed and cheaper rates. According to an article from CNBC, *"In the United States, people on average produce about seventy-five pounds of textile waste each year, according to EPA (Environmental Protection Agency). The Ellen MacArthur Foundation estimates that about $500 billion is lost each year as a result of clothing being thrown out instead of being reused or recycled."* According to the *NY Times* article: *"The United States as a whole wastes more than $160 billion in food a year. Globally, we throw out about 1.3 billion tons of food a year, a third of all the food we grow. Food waste and loss has a huge carbon footprint: 3.3 billion tons of carbon equivalent."* Can someone please explain to me, with all that we are wasting, why we are destroying our rainforests for more space for food and commerce?

Get my point: see through the illusion, scarcity is all-consuming! This isn't abundance, this is waste. Fear of not enough. We are so scared that we are not going to have enough that we're willing to buy more than we need and then throw out close to half of it! Scarcity has us buying more and more while we let the real things in life, the priceless ones, the ones that are free, just disappear and are undervalued: love, people, connection, nature, kindness, laughter, happiness, space and wellbeing. It's time to wake up from the illusion of scarcity before Mother Nature does it for us.

Scarcity is thinking there is never enough.
Never enough time.
Never enough money.
Never enough love.
Never enough pleasure.
Never enough _____
What is your never enough?

Scarcity traps you in the illusion of a future happiness. I invite you to jump out of the hamster wheel and see that happiness is ready and available to you right here and right now. Remember, if you are breathing, you are worthy. You validate your worth, not money or people. Where do you want to create from? Scarcity or Abundance? Say yes to this new reality and begin to see all the magic that exists around you.

The power is yours and you get to choose the narrative you want to build your life on. All it takes is seeing all that exists in your life. It's not the car, the house, the vacation or whatever external thing you believe will make you happy. Happiness exists in the present moment. It's when you choose to pause and see everything all around you, RIGHT NOW. Abundance is choosing to put your energy, words and focus on all you have, internally. Once you turn that light switch on, you see more of what you have, not what you do not.

Here is a **Gratitude Practice Worksheet** for you to use as a tool to train your eyes on seeing all that you have. You are working that abundance muscle by using this worksheet. Every day, you will train the abundance muscle to see five things you are grateful for. At the end of every month, you'll use this muscle to write down what you've accomplished in the month, what fun things you've done and what you are grateful for.

GRATITUDE PRACTICE WORKSHEET

Daily Gratitude's
Use this section to celebrate the simple, spectacular moments in your life.

I am grateful for....
1. I am grateful for the air I breathe.
2. I am grateful for my life.
3. I am grateful for the delicious taste of ice cream.
4. I am grateful for the blue sky outside.

Joy Tips:
A scarcity mindset has your attention and focus on everything you do not have. An abundant mindset has your attention and focus on all that you do have. This is the difference between a scarcity mindset versus an abundant mindset.

Being grateful allows you to feel the joy of simple moments.
It trains your mind in seeing all there is in your life
versus seeing all you do not have.

Abundance is present when all relations are honored as sacred
and when gratitude is expressed to every living part of creation.

Monthly Gratitude's
Use the section below to celebrate all you accomplished in a month by writing down actions you've taken that you are proud of, then reflect back on them at the end of the month to celebrate yourself and your magnificence.

January: *I increased my Savings One account, I bought myself flowers.*

February: *I set up auto-pay on all my fixed expenses, I went for a walk in nature.*

March: *I took the time out to do my morning ritual most mornings this month.*

Joy Tip:
Keep mementos from the year in a box to celebrate
and reflect on at the end of the year.

"If the only prayer you ever say in your entire life is Thank You,
it will be enough."

– Meister Eckhart

----

*To download a blank version of the gratitude practice worksheet go to **www.toniag.com/rich-resources**

By writing down 5 things you are grateful for each day, you are claiming at the start of the day that you choose to root yourself in abundance. It's an important practice to do because when you step out the door and out into the world, scarcity still prevails. It's up to you to shine your abundance light. Every month, to anchor into even more abundance because you can tend to forget what you've accomplished along the way, fill in the things you are grateful for that happened in that month. This sheet is a great way to remind you to pause and celebrate what you've accomplished. Every couple of months, look at what you wrote down to take stock of all your hard work. Then at the end of the year, you see clearly the growth in your journey, and all the baby steps that lead you to where you are now.

Celebrate it and get used to the feeling of celebrating your greatness. You are operating from abundance and love. Congratulations on having the awareness to choose where you make decisions from, scarcity or abundance. Any time you feel disconnected from your source of abundance, go outside and let nature show you the way back. I know for me, anytime I go outside I feel rich. Every time I see and sniff a flower I am reminded, *"Holy crap, look how beautiful that flower is, it's magnificent and I'm connected to that magnificence."* If I am connected to that Source, how can I not create my reality the way that I want it?

> **FUN TIP:** Get outside in nature and notice all the Earth's abundance reflected in the world around you. This could take the form of marveling at the tapestry of leaves adorning the trees, or the carpet of wildflowers in your local park, because it symbolizes the generosity and bounty provided by Mother Earth.

Tonia's Mini Money Life Lessons

The Voice of Scarcity

My scarcity side still comes out. My fear, doubt, worry and self-sabotage. My moody self and how inconsistent I can be. One moment/day I'm super happy and have complete clarity and then the next day, I'm negative, wanting to hide and not see anyone. I dislike my needy side and my lazy side. The side that doesn't want to do anything and wants to just avoid life. My victim side. Not wanting to be bothered with anyone or with life. I feel disconnected and disappointed with the world we live in. Racism, inequality, poverty, disease, illness, war, greed. People literally work themselves to death. Working so hard for material things. I feel like I don't belong in this world. I feel disconnected because the majority of people are living in the illusion. At times I get disappointed in myself because I get brought back into the illusion. I desire and want money. I get stressed out about having enough of it or if I can create it. Believing that this new abundant world I live in is really true, or am I just fucking crazy? Can I live in the world of trust, faith and surrender when it comes to money? I really do believe that yes, I can.

Sustainability

The word "sustainability" has been the motivation for so much of my work in uncovering why my clients/people in general cannot sustain healthy money habits. I have spent countless time creating beautiful money systems for people only to find they've reverted to their old ways of handling money or really, not handling it at all. Why are new habits so difficult to maintain? How do I create sustainable money relationships for people? The hard truth is I can't, no one can. That's why I said at the beginning of this stage that the grand joke is that the money system doesn't create lasting peace of mind, freedom, security, or independence. You have to want it for yourself.

According to dictionary.com, sustainability has two definitions: *"The ability to be sustained, supported, upheld or confirmed. Environmental Science. The quality of not being harmful to the environment or depleting natural resources, and thereby supporting long-term ecological balance."* Sustainability is contingent on support. It's the support that makes it long term and not just a passing phase. I've created some tools to support you in sustaining your healthy money habits and putting into practice the money system you developed over the previous three stages. This allows you to maintain your healthy relationship with money and become your own money guru. The clearer you are on what you want, the easier it is for the universe to give you what you are asking for.

The first tool I'm sharing allows you to get clear about the amount of money you want to manifest and is from the book *Think and Grow Rich* by Napoleon Hill. It's a money mantra statement. By using this statement daily, you affirm the amount of money that's on its way to you. The second tool we're using are money dates. Yep, you heard me. Money dates. These are days within the month that you schedule time with yourself to manage your money and pay your bills. They are dates because you make them fun, not this dreary task you have to do, which may have been the old way you approached handling your money.

Let's start with the money mantra statement. The focus is being grateful for what you have, accepting where you are with your current income, and putting your power of thought behind creating the income you desire. I made some modifications to the statement adding in (of course) some joy and gratitude. Mainly, I'm using the format given by Napoleon Hill, who was inspired to write his book by Andrew Carnegie's magic formula for success. He created quite a bit of wealth in his time so I do believe in the power of this statement and of course use it for myself!

MONEY MANTRA WORKSHEET

"By _____ (date), I will have in my possession _____ (amount of money), which will come to me in various amounts from time to time during the interim and I'm so grateful for it.

I see the amazing clients and/or employers I get to co-create with who are jumping with joy to pay me for my gifts. In return for this money, I will give the most efficient service of which I am capable, providing the best possible quantity and quality of service in the capacity as a (whatever it is you are, coach etc.) of (describe the service or merchandise you intend to sell).

I believe that I will have this money in my possession. My faith is so strong that I can now see this money before my eyes. I can touch it with my hands. It is now awaiting transfer to me at the time, and in the proportion that I deliver the service I intend to provide in return for it. I am awaiting a plan by which to accumulate this money, I will follow, and act on that plan when it is received."

"The more you look for synchronicity, the more magical your life becomes. You are the magician that makes the grass green."

- Robert Anton Wilson

---

*To download a blank version of the money mantra worksheet go to
www.toniag.com/rich-resources

When filling in the blanks to the money mantra statement, fear can arise and have you afraid to write down your answers, to ask for what you want, or believe it will come true. This fear can show up in the form of your old friend "I don't know" as a story, blocking you from filling out the statement. To stay stuck in "I don't know" is a lot more convenient than to believe in yourself and the power you have to create the life you want. Here's what it can sound like: "*I don't know what services to offer. I don't know how much I want to make. I don't know when to make it by.*" The truth is you do know and fear is normal when doing something new, so you make friends with it by thanking the fear, not shaming it. You have all the answers to fill in the above lines. Let's review what to fill in on your money mantra statement and begin using your powers of creating for the income you desire.

First, fill in the blank space for the *date*. It can be monthly, quarterly or yearly. The trick is to start listening to yourself and going with the one that feels good for you. It will feel both frightening and possible at the same time. The second line is *amount of money*. You figured this number out in Stage Two, Foundation, on the **Expense Organization Worksheet.** Find the row for *total of fixed, variable, & fun expenses* and this amount is your base number. Next, add in the amounts you were short of money for. For example, more money for savings, vacations, food or anything else and add these numbers to the base total you just got from the **Expense Organization Worksheet**. Like the date, you want it to feel frightening and possible at the same time.

Now, you have your amount and it's not just this arbitrary number you pulled from the sky, like six figures or seven figures. This number is connected to things that will bring real value into your life to fuel your manifestation with the power of desire. I cannot stand when I hear businesses using an income of six or seven figures as a marketing tool, insinuating that your life will be better once you make this income. No, it won't. Money makes things more convenient, but it's not happiness. There is nothing wrong with making six or seven figures and desiring this. Please do. I want you to. It's been far too long that we have had an unequal distribution of wealth in this country and world. Get that money, but also have the dollar amount you are calling in be connected to items and experiences that will add value to your life, not proving your value by the amount of money you have or make.

On the third line, put down your job title or what you call yourself when providing this service. On the fourth line, put down the services you're giving in exchange for this money. It's in the giving that we receive. What you give out is what you get back. If you have your own business or are an entrepreneur, what gifts are you offering to the world? If you have a job, what services are you offering your employer?

When I realized I wanted to start my own business, I asked myself the question, *"When I'm bored or stressed out, what things or hobbies do I find myself doing?"* A memory popped into my mind of me in my room the day after 9/11. I saw myself walking over to my dresser, opening the first drawer, and looking at all my undergarments folded perfectly and color coordinated! My entire room was organized like this. I thought, *"If I used organizing to calm me down on the worst day of my life, imagine how much I'll enjoy doing it on the good days."* The bonus was that I already knew I would like it on the bad days. Next, I made sure there was a market for this by asking myself was there a problem I was solving for the consumer and would they pay for it? Yes and yes. I solved the problem of disorganization and in return I got money for it. It was a win/win. That's how I chose starting a business of being a professional organizer.

And if you're not happy with your job, use this statement to call in the opportunities to get paid for what you enjoy doing. Allow yourself to play with options, to discover what excites you and follow your curiosity on what that is. What allows you to shine your light, share your brilliance and put that gift out into the world? Put it out there in the universe.

If you find yourself stuck on what to offer, ask yourself the below questions to support you in discovering what that is.

When you're bored or stressed out, what things or hobbies do you find yourself doing?
What lights you up?
What do you love to do?
What would you never get sick of doing?
What things do you do hobby-wise?
What things in the world make you angry that you would like to change?
What brings you joy whenever you do it?

"Find your gift and deliver it to as many people as possible."

- Tony Robbins

Now, look over your answers to these questions and notice if there is a recurring theme coming through. Maybe something in there jumps out at you that you would enjoy doing. Is there a way to turn it into something you can offer and receive money in exchange for it? When putting offers out into the world, shift into a mentality of abundance by going for the triple win. Ask yourself, *"Is this good for me, good for the other person, and good for the whole of humanity?"* If yes, you have an abundance trifecta!

For anyone who is looking for ways to make an extra income, use these questions to support you in finding out what that can be. A simple way to make money is selling things on the various platforms that exist online or through consignment shops. Nowadays, people seem to have too many things. I know, I was the one they called to organize it all and make it fit in their spaces. You ever realize how many companies have sprung up that sell storage? Yes, a place for you to store all your stuff, that you probably will never use, and you pay for it monthly. So sell it. Make money off it.

The freedom you created in your mental space, you want to create in your physical space as well. So, get rid of things you no longer use and not just by throwing them out! Take it one step further and ask yourself, *"Is this something I can sell, donate, or trash?"* If you can sell it, put that money to paying down your debt, if no debt, split it with your savings and Fun Debit account. Enjoy that money. If it's something you cannot sell, then donate it! There are plenty of places like Housing Works which will reuse your stuff.

Here's a fun tip if you're worried about parting with certain things: tell yourself the joy it brought you can now be given to someone else in the act of giving it away. Donating allows you to spread joy and you get a charitable donation receipt for all those things, so you can write them off on your taxes. Win/win/win. Give with joy, people. If it's trash, first see if it can be recycled before you put it in the regular garbage. It's all about sustainability. Be kind to our Mother Nature, she gives us so much – let's give back to her too.

Have fun and get creative with how you can bring in more money. Read the money mantra statement every morning and night to affirm the money on its way to you. Keep it by your nightstand so you remember to read it or put it by your toothbrush. Nothing wrong with using habits already in place to anchor in the new ones. While you are reading it envision that amount of money sitting in your bank account. Allow that feeling of having that money wash over you. You got this!

Tonia's Mini Money Message
Money is working for you now,
you are not working for money!

You've learned a lot of new habits, tools, and worksheets to use when it comes to your money. So, now what? How do you sustain your healthy new money habits and put into practice the money system you developed over the previous three stages? How do you make this relationship with money last and not just be another passing phase? With support and you do this by having money dates with yourself. That's right, Money Dates! Money is working for you now, you are not working for money and as a result, you commit to managing it. Your money dates are how you manage your money and in order to make it stick we add some fun! Nobody wants to be on a boring date, not even your money! To add fun and play to your money dates, create a money playlist to jazz it up. On the days you really don't want to do the money dates, get dressed up sexy to get yourself psyched up to do them – why not, you're worth it! Add the element of play in. Sometimes in life things aren't the most fun to do but you learn to bring in the elements of joy and play to turn a mundane task into something exciting. That's why there's a whole stage dedicated to Fun to support you in sustaining a joyful relationship with money.

Another reason people get stuck on continuing to manage their money is because they don't know what to do. Well, problem solved – below is the omega, the **Money Date Checklist**. It is your map key for your money system. This way you know exactly which worksheets to use for each money category and from what stage. This way, you can nurture your new relationship with money and enjoy your intimate time with it.

MONEY DATE CHECKLIST

What to Do:
How often will you have a money date with yourself: weekly, bi-weekly, monthly?
Weekly
What day of the week feels good to have your money date?
Thursday
What time of day is best for you to have your money date?
6pm
What does your money date consist of doing? (Here is a list to use on your money dates.)

MONEY DATE CHECKLIST

Mindset

☑ I updated my wins and my losses on my **Gratitude Worksheet** /spreadsheet for this month.

Date I updated my celebrations: 4/1.

Accounts

☑ I updated my balances on my **Accounts Action Worksheet** /spreadsheet for this month.

Date I updated my balances: 3/25.

Debt

☑ I updated my balances on my **Debt Actions Worksheet** / spreadsheet for this month.

Date I updated my balances: 4/1.

Expenses

☑ I reviewed my **Fixed Expense Action Worksheet**/spreadsheet to see what is due.

☑ I paid the bills that are due for this month and checked them off the list.

Date I last paid my bills: 3/25.

MONEY DATE CHECKLIST

Income

☑ I followed my **Income Actions Worksheet**/spreadsheet and transferred my income to its designated accounts aka *money homes.*

Date I last transferred my income: 3/25.

Savings

☑ I reviewed my **Savings Action Worksheet** to keep my eye on the prize with my savings aims.

Date I last reviewed my savings numbers: 4/1.

Inspired Action Items

☑ I looked at the list of items I will complete and took action on one item this week.

"Infinite Spirit, open the way for the Divine Design of my life to manifest; let the genius within me now be released; let me see clearly the perfect plan."

- The Game of Life, Florence Shinn

---

*To download a blank version of the money date checklist go to **www.toniag.com/rich-resources**

This is a suggested outline for you to use on your money dates. Set a day and a time to sit with your money worksheets and update them. How long you have these money dates for depends on you and what works best for you. Currently, I have weekly money dates with myself for an hour every Thursday. I have separate dates for my business and personal money stuff. Every week they appear in my Google calendar automatically. As you get more comfortable having these dates with money, you will find that some sheets you may not need any more, or maybe there are some new ones you want to add in. Go for it! This is all about you having the tools that best serve you to manage your money. At times I don't always show up excited to have my money dates. That's why I have fun hacks for them to motivate me when I'm not in the mood because it happens. I have a money playlist I specifically listen to for my money dates. The first song is always one that gets me pumped up (one being A Deeper Love by Aretha Franklin). Another thing I do is use color pens for figuring out my numbers on paper and for my notes. Also, my spreadsheets are colorful so they are pleasant on the eyes and fun to look at. Allow the above worksheet to support you in managing your money and think of the ways you will bring in the elements of fun and play to your money dates.

Celebration moment! You made it through sustainability. This is a very big deal! Work the system and if you detour off the road, it's okay. Now that you're taking consistent action on the plan laid out for you with your money, things will come up – your emotions will arise and fear can show up. We want it to, welcome that fear. Befriend it. Listen to it and release it. Do not be mean to your emotions. If you are, you're still rejecting parts of yourself. Forgive yourself and start where you last left off. The reality is that this will take time, so be patient and loving with yourself as these new habits get formed. Take a moment and have some fun to congratulate yourself!

> **FUN TIP:** Take yourself out on a date and go and do something fun. Go have coffee at a cool cafe, go to a museum you've been wanting to check out, have a glass of wine in a beautiful place, get your favorite treat from a bakery. Whatever works for you. Treat yourself. You deserve it!

Mind

On this leg of the journey you will learn to use your greatest asset, YOU: because if you do not learn mastery over yourself, you are not going to learn mastery over anything. Doing this allows you to sustain an abundant life using yourself as your greatest tool. Learning how to surrender, trust and have faith in the universe's plan for you is what allows you to be in flow with life. But, how do you surrender? Is trust something that is easy for you? What do I mean by faith? What plan are you trusting in? Well, we learn the answer to all these questions when we have an authentic relationship with ourselves that includes our mind, bodies and soul. Next, we'll discover the tools to have this relationship so we can sustain happiness in our own lives. Let's start with diving into the power of your mind.

The whole aim is to surrender your mind to your heart, so that your heart is calling the shots. Your mind is then being used as the great assistant it is by taking action on the heart's desires. When you do this, the world is your oyster. As a controller, perfectionist, and overthinker, this wasn't an easy concept for me to embrace. My heart was locked away and I always acted from logic. When I was told to surrender my mind, it went into overdrive wondering, *"What does surrender mean? How do I surrender? What are the steps so I can surrender?"* The mind always wants to know how and the "how" kills creation.

Creation is messy and she does not follow the rules of how or when. Thus, practicing surrendering my mind to my heart was one of the hardest things for me to do because it involved me embracing my vulnerability and releasing control. As a recovering controller and perfectionist, every morning I say a mantra to remind me to do this (in the soul section I share this mantra). Since I have, my life has yielded me so much freedom.

Surrendering is such a powerful act because what we are doing is releasing control, which allows for more possibilities and goodness to come into our lives. When we try, push and control, we are not allowing for life's possibilities to come through – actually, we are pushing them away. Practicing detachment and acceptance will support you in surrendering the mind. Let's go deeper into these principles so we can understand how the mind tries to keep control over us and how to use our breath to support us in having mastery over our minds.

Detachment

Being attached to our external identities and to the outcome of results in our lives is what can keep us afraid of the unknown. It allows external things like jobs, homes, cars, family, kids, etc. to validate who we are on the inside. We stay attached to these identities, because who are we without our jobs? If not a mother or father, daughter or son? It's this attachment to all these external things and identities that causes the emotional pain in our lives versus letting it go with love. It allows us to hold on to things and circumstances longer than we are meant to. Attachment goes against the natural cycles of life, death and rebirth. Change is the only constant, attachment is not real. It's a construct of the ego to keep us safe and still. Protecting us from stepping out of the box and learning to get uncomfortable with life. Attachment keeps us playing small.

When you gather the courage to step out of your box, you learn that nothing external validates who you are: *you* validate who you are. It's a job from the inside out and it begins with letting go of what no longer serves you, with grace and love. This opens up the space in your life to receive the greatness on its way. You create the space to let the new in. The beauty, the possibilities and the wonder of life exist in the void and in the darkness. The unknown and life's mysteries are where the juiciness of life live.

Nothing ever stays the same. Nature shows you that. What if you walked around detached from your external identity and trusted in the abundance of life? Imam Al-Shafi'i says it perfectly, so imagine walking around embracing this concept: *"My heart is at ease knowing that what was meant for me will never miss me, and that what misses me was never meant for me."* How beautiful is that? People, places and objects in our lives leave because they have had their time and served their purpose in our growth. Actually, holding on is what stunts our growth.

Life is all about growing and learning. Thus, you release form and invite in being, consciousness, and awareness. Operating from your heart and being present. For a moment, let go of the lists, the "to-dos," and allow yourself to just BE. Being is allowing yourself to do nothing so you can feel everything, resulting in connection to your inner truth or authentic self. From this space, you will be shown what to do next and take action from your heart instead of your head. Let go of caring what people think or dreaming too big because it will be too difficult. These are the things and thoughts that block you from dreaming or allowing yourself to be abundant. While you are releasing attachment, you are learning to accept all of who you are. Don Miguel Ruiz has a beautiful self-forgiveness prayer you can use to practice this concept (in Resources section of this book). Let's move along now to learn about acceptance.

Acceptance

Another principle that will support you in surrendering wholeheartedly is acceptance. Acceptance of who you are, where you are, and all that's surrounding you. It's giving yourself the approval that *you are enough*. That all of you is enough. Coming to peace with your past and knowing where you are right now is perfect. Acceptance is about loving all of you – the good, the bad and the ugly. The shadow and the light sides.

When I allowed myself to go into the dark places within myself, I learned something – something very powerful that would further change the way I viewed my negative emotions. The darkness within me wasn't bad, like all the portrayals of the dark imply. It was a *place* within me, within my soul, that I chose to ignore and hide away. They were pieces of myself that I jailed because they were judged as not pretty or proper. The dark places aren't evil; they are places within myself that no longer wanted to be ignored and alone in the dark. They wanted the lights turned on. The pain, the hurt, and the anxiety are just the messengers to get our attention for the pieces within ourselves that we repressed and shamed. All they want is our love and acceptance.

Inviting our emotions from our unconscious to our conscious mind is where true independence lies and is what releases these emotions. When you turn on the lights for all parts of you to be seen, it gives you permission to shine that light out into the world being authentically you. All it takes is flipping that switch on. Becoming friends with your emotions and no longer allowing fear to run the show is how you begin to have mastery over them (not control) and life becomes this playful space of learning and fun.

Being in the FLOW means LOVING all versions of you and KNOWING what all these versions of yourself are. It's inviting the one-person show that exists in your mind to reveal itself to you (I'm still getting introduced to new characteristics from my one-woman mind show). It's becoming truly intimate with who you are on the inside and getting acquainted with the "me" show.

Surrender to your greatness and embrace the gift of acceptance that causes your current circumstances to be good. To support you in stepping into this greatness is learning to use your breath to release your emotions, accept all of you, and gain control of your mind.

Tool: Breathwork

Ever notice when someone is having a panic attack the first thing they're given is a bag to slow down their breath? Ever wonder why they do this? During a panic attack, that's the mind racing with fear, doubt, worry (an all-out assault on the mind) which then causes the breath to start racing the same way. The bag allows for the breath to be controlled and slowed down. Once the breath slows down, so does the mind. Your breath is the vehicle for controlling your mind. When you master your breath, you master your mind and learn to surrender the mind to the desires of the heart.

Your breath is so powerful and is literally your life force that you could not live without. You have this amazing tool available to you right now that you may have not been taught to take advantage of. Talk about moving out of the lens of scarcity and into abundance. When you breathe with awareness, you access the magic of the present moment and the gift that it is. Your breath is the gateway to this moment, to The Now, and a tool to use to connect you to the truest form of self. A breath I use all the time is the "calming", which takes you out of fight-or-flight response. This way when you make a decision, it is not coming from desperation. Anytime you find yourself freaking out, nervous and needing to calm down, use this breath. You can do it anywhere and it's simple to do.

Lets practice this "calming" breath together. All the breathing is done through the nose and for a count of four. This slows down your breath and brings your mind back to the present moment. You can find the audio of this on my website, at (www.toniag.com /rich-resources).

Close your eyes.
Breathe in through your nose for 1, 2, 3, 4.
Hold the inhale for 1, 2, 3, 4.
Exhale through your nose for 1, 2, 3, 4.
Hold the exhale for 1, 2, 3, 4.
Continue with this breath for 1-3 minutes.

How do you feel after that? Do you find yourself more relaxed, grounded, and centered? Take a pause and notice how you are feeling.

Here is a **Breathwork Sheet**, which lists all the breathwork I use in my daily life to breathe through negative emotions or thoughts when they come up and are great to use when that money pain shows up. Using breathwork is a tool to transmute that pain and a way to move it through your body. Each breathwork exercise lists what it does, the benefit, how to do it, and a suggestion on how to end the breath to anchor yourself. Practice them, see how you feel when you do them.

You can see from the benefits which breath will serve you best to support you in moving through the challenge you are facing. Do you desire for your emotions to be balanced? Do you desire to release the fear rising up in you when wanting to take forward action? Do you desire to be grounded before a big meeting or decision? Do you desire to cool yourself off when you're all hot and bothered? Well, there's a breath for all of these situations and they are listed below. Have fun experimenting with them. Go within, connect to the power of now and receive your infinite intelligence.

BREATHWORK SHEET

Name: Emotions Balancer
Time: 1 minute

Benefits
Gets rid of unhealthy emotions & impatience. The chest and the lungs are the balance center, so this breath helps you live life from a place of balance so that you can be neutral.

Directions
Breathe only into the upper chest area.
Inhale for 3 counts and exhale for 2 counts through the nose (you can use the count "1-2-3" for the inhale, "1-2" for the exhale).
Keep your eyes open and look at a focal point ahead.

BREATHWORK SHEET

Name: Fear Buster
Time: 1 minute

Benefits
Rejuvenates the body.
Gets rid of fear from life.
Grounds you.

Directions
Breathe only into the lower stomach area.
Inhale for 3 counts and exhale for 2 counts through the nose (you can use the cue "1-2-3" for the inhale, "1-2" for the exhale).
Keep your eyes open and look at a focal point ahead.

Name: Grounds You
Time: 3 minutes

Benefits
Takes you out of the 'fight or flight' mindset. Allows you to be non-reactive.

Directions
Inhale for a count of 4 (1-2-3-4)
Hold the inhale for a count of 4 (1-2-3-4)
Exhale for a count of 4 (1-2-3-4)
Hold the exhale for a count of 4 (1-2-3-4)
Eyes can be open or closed.

BREATHWORK SHEET

Name: Calms You
Time: 3 minutes

Benefits
Cools your body down as well as your emotions. Brings you blessings.

Directions
Inhale through a curled tongue and exhale through your nose. If it is not possible to curl the sides of the tongue up, place the tip of the tongue behind the front upper teeth. Inhale through the sides of the tongue and exhale through the nose.
Breath in and out in equal breaths of 4.

All above Breaths
Finish each breath: inhale deeply through the nose, hold the breath in and bring the tongue to the roof of the mouth, then exhale through the mouth.

"My heart is at ease knowing that
what was meant for me will never miss me, and that
what misses me was never meant for me."

- Imam Al-Shafi'i

---

*To download a blank version of the breathwork sheet go to
www.toniag.com/rich-resources

The intention is to surrender the mind to act on behalf of the heart, not the ego. The breath is what controls the mind. Master your breath and you master your mind.

Let me share a story with you on how I used breathwork to support me in finishing this book. When working on this book there were many moments that I walked away from writing or getting into a flow with it because it meant I had to push through the discomfort of being scared to reveal my vulnerabilities and speak my truth about money. I resisted discipline because in the majority of self-help and leadership workshops I attended, they taught me to just push through the pain and discomfort. Do whatever it takes! I did and I manipulated life because of it. I was a robot who just did, did, did and exercised nothing but discipline. I now resisted using it out of fear of becoming that robot again, but I realized I had to form a new relationship and distinction of it if I wanted to finish this book in my lifetime. So I did, discipline is good and necessary when it is used in alignment with my true essence and soul.

The ah-hah came when I was writing and hit a thick wall of overwhelm. I didn't have the energy to push through it. As I surrendered to that realization, I heard it: *"Don't push through, breathe through."* It's like a switch went on and a clear distinction appeared in my mind. My inner wisdom showing me the way. Breathing through is leaning into the discomfort and allowing the feelings to work their way through my body, to come up and out, not to suppress them. It comes from a place of compassion and love. Pushing through is ignoring the discomfort and squashing these feelings deep down into my body, hiding them away, suppressing them. It comes from a place of control and being unloving towards myself. Pushing through is restraining and forceful, breathing through is releasing and allowing. This journey is all about growth and releasing what no longer serves, not burying it. When you feel yourself being confronted and hitting that wall of *too much*, remember to just breathe through it.

Body

Our bodies are the vehicles to connect us to our intuition and power. They have so much to teach us about the strength, love, power and infinite wisdom that exists within us. When we learn to tune in to this voice of inner wisdom we develop a trust within ourselves and to our power. If we do not trust in ourselves it holds so much power over our lives because we can only trust others in the capacity that we trust ourselves. When we do not trust in others or ourselves, it is a very skeptical, lonely and hard world out there. We have to do everything on our own and that's a scarcity mindset. We are no longer subscribing to that mindset. Moving forward, it's all about abundance and support.

Let's learn to develop a deeper relationship to self that's built on trust. Thus allowing us to trust in the process and plan of life because we know no matter the circumstances, we have the answers within ourselves to figure it out. All things are working in our favor and for our good. Throughout this category we will learn how to put boundaries in place, to ask for what we want, to receive and give graciously so we can feel safe in speaking our truth and trust in the divine wisdom that exists within our bodies. We will also learn to use meditation as the hotline to connect to this inner truth. It's a return home to ourselves.

Boundaries

When you feel pain in your life, the pain is there to get your attention to show you that something in your life is not working. Boundaries are the actions you put in place from the lesson you learned from that painful experience so you do not go down that road again. This action is what allows you to not be controlled or manipulated. Your boundaries allow you to feel safe in your body, because you trust you can speak your truth with conviction about your needs. When you honor your truth, you begin to develop the relationship with trusting yourself.

A big lesson that I learned is that I didn't trust others because I didn't trust myself. I was too busy trying to be perfect and pleasing others by saying yes to everything, even if I didn't want to do it. The intention behind my actions was proving my worth and worthiness by how much I did and gave. I was saying yes to things and then resenting the person or experience after. I'm exhausted just thinking about it. I had to learn to say no to things I didn't want to do and not worry about what others would think. The point was to honor my truth, and for you to honor *your* truth by saying NO to the things you do not want to do and YES to the things you want do and putting boundaries in place so you have the time to do those things. Below, I'm sharing the strategies I used when first learning to put boundaries into practice in my life – these worked and are priceless! The first has to do with emotional boundaries and the second is for physical boundaries.

My aunt, Tami Coyne – who is a spiritual coach/counselor, certified Spiritual Response Therapy consultant, medium and all-round kick-ass human being, gave the first strategy to me.

Boundaries were quite difficult for me, because not only was it hard for me to say no, but also I was unaware that I was an empath (I was picking up on every emotion and feeling around me) so I couldn't distinguish which feelings were mine and which belonged to others. I couldn't identify what boundary I really wanted to put in place. During one of our sessions, Tami gave me this great visualization to practice to support me with this, which I share with you here:

> *First, close your eyes. I want you to imagine yourself and the person you want to put boundaries in place with. Then, imagine there is a wall between the two of you. Next, I want you to begin a conversation with this person and envision a can getting thrown over the wall every time either of you say something. Lastly, when that can comes over the wall, I want you to look at it and distinguish: Are these words in this can useful to me or is it trash? If it's useful, you keep it, and if it's trash, you throw it back over the wall and back over to that person. It is not your garbage to keep if it doesn't serve you. It is that simple to put boundaries in place, you just throw that trash back over the wall. Now, open your eyes.*

When I opened my eyes, it's as if I was seeing a new world. What a concept. I did not have to carry the baggage of others. It's not my responsibility. It was not mine and so I could throw those cans right over the wall. This allowed me to put into place the boundary of not taking on other people's trash. It just makes me dirty, smelly and heavy! It also made me mindful of my words and the trash I throw over to people with my words. It put things into perspective and had me being very intentional with the things I say and the words I use.

How much garbage have you collected over the years by taking on the unhelpful words of others and allowing them to penetrate your mind with their trash? I know when I realized this, I had a whole dump's worth! This is why I was so tired and exhausted after talking to some people. I was choosing to take on their trash. Well, not anymore, we are not anyone's trash receptacle. That's why we have boundaries because our time is one of our most precious commodities. We don't have the time to be weighed down by other people's garbage! When you go out into the world, this is a great tool to arm yourself with when people throw their scarcity stories at you; you can throw it back over the wall and continue living in abundance. So, let's learn the second exercise to use for you to get clarity on what boundaries you desire in your physical life.

Tonia's Mini Money Message
We are not anyone's trash receptacle.

Joy Tip:
Envision this as your bubble of protection (like Glenda the good witch in the Wizard of Oz). This is your happy place bubble. Stay consistent in these actions and feel free to adjust them when other things you would like to change come up.

BOUNDARIES EXERCISE

Steps:

1. Chose an aspect of your life that you would like to improve: work, health, relationships, money or self-care.

2. In the left column, write all the things you are no longer willing to experience in the chosen aspect of your life.

3. In the circle write down actions you will take in order to no longer be affected by the list outside the circle. The outside list is what's holding you back from attaining the life you desire. These actions in the circle create your protective boundaries.

Chosen life aspect: Self-care

I am no longer willing to experience....
- Doubting and not trusting myself.
- Being disorganized with my money.
- Over thinking and worrying.
- Feeling tired in my body and disconnected from nature.

What I Desire.....
- Meditate in the morning.
- To have my money dates every week.
- Journal everyday.
- Go for a walk outside everyday.

*To download a blank version of the boundaries exercise go to **www.toniag.com/rich-resources**

"Freedom means the capability to say yes when yes is needed, to say no when no is needed, & sometimes to keep quiet when nothing is needed – to be silent, not to say anything. When all these dimensions are available, there is freedom."

- Osho

Okay, you now have the actions for the boundaries to put in place in your life. It's up to you to be in integrity with yourself and do what you say you are going to do. Oh – and when you don't, please just forgive yourself and pick up where you last left off. Don't sprinkle shame, guilt, judgment and all these self-sabotaging things on top of it. Don't complicate it by beating yourself up. Making mistakes is natural and an integral part of the learning process. In fact, I want you to celebrate yourself when you make these mistakes, have a party! These mistakes show you that you're going for it. It's possible if you're not making mistakes, you're playing it safe. Accept wherever you're at, love up on it and jump back on the horse when you fall off. Vince Lombardi says it best: *"It's not whether you get knocked down. It's whether you get up."* This is what an abundant mindset is all about. Accepting all of you. Being kind to yourself because you are worth it. You have the forgiveness sheets from the Freedom stage to support you when you need them. Next, you are learning to ask for what you want in your life.

Asking for What You Want

One of the things that requires putting boundaries in place is having the courage to speak your truth and ask for what you want. This simple act takes you out of victim mode and puts you in a place of empowerment. No more complaining, *"Oh this is hard, I have to do this all on my own, this is taking so much time to do!"* It removes all that. You can ask others and the universe for what you want and desire help with. It can feel vulnerable to put yourself in a position where you are giving someone the power to say "yes" or "no" to you. One reason we resist asking is fear of rejection. *"What if the other person says no? What if I inconvenience someone else, what if, what if, what if?"* If you are someone who doesn't have boundaries in your life, you will worry about inconveniencing others, since you assume (as the saying goes: you make an ass out of you and me) they can't say no because you can't say no. What's going on internally for yourself, you project externally to others. You're flipping the script on NO and taking your power back by asking for what you want.

Let's begin by unraveling all the crap we attach to the no. First, when someone says no, they are not rejecting you. It's not about you. They are honoring themselves in what they want and do not want. Second, a no can also be no for *right now*. Let go of the attachment that they are saying no to you personally – again, it's not about you and who you are. Third, if possible, flip it on its head and celebrate the person for being able to articulate what they want and do not want. Celebrate the no. Have you ever seen a kid getting dragged to a doctor's appointment that they didn't want to go to? That's what it feels like being with a person who said yes out of guilt. Own the gift of the no. Fourth, each *"no"* brings you closer to the genuine "*hell, yes!*" The genuine hell yes is so much sweeter to be with then someone who wanted to say no but felt bad to do so.

Asking for what you want has you standing in a place of empowerment. Ask yourself, do you want to go through life as a victim or empowered? What ground are you choosing to stand on? When you own your no, it makes it easier for you to celebrate the No of others. You can than see it's just them articulating their boundaries of what they want and do not want. Yes to that!

Today, I want you to go out and practice asking for what you want. Start small. It can be asking someone to hold the door open for you. Asking for someone to grab something off the shelf that you could reach yourself but it's difficult. Ask someone else for the time when you need it, even though there's a phone in your pocket or a watch on your wrist.

Ask for anything! If you like to challenge yourself, put into practice asking for something every day. Start exercising that asking muscle. The words must get out of your head and into reality. It's in the ask that you receive. What does that mean? When you are asking for what you want and have the courage to say it out loud, it's not just that person who is hearing your ask – the universe is too. The universe wants to give you everything you want, but – are you in a place of receiving it? So let's talk about getting ourselves into receptive mode to receive all this goodness that we are asking for. What's something you can ask for today?

Receiving

If we truly want to create and grow in our lives, we must expand our capacity to receive. For some of us, it can be a difficult thing to receive without expectation. Without expectation means releasing the attachment to it coming in a specific way and staying open to the other avenues it can come from. That's why detaching from the no is so important. Even if that person says no, it doesn't mean it's not coming. A great book to tune us into hearing the universe is *E-Squared* by Pam Grout. She gives quick, easy and fun experiments to do that show us exactly how the universe responds to what we ask.

This happened to me when I was looking for an apartment in Brooklyn. I sucked at asking for help. This is a muscle that I continuously have to work. I was on the beach with two of my friends (one of whom I've known since I was 6), Lisa and Raquel, talking to them about looking for an apartment and my desires for the apartment. I wanted it in a private home, I wanted the rent to be no more than $1,000, one bedroom, a place for me to put my desk to work, etc. I was clear on the vision of what I wanted. Then, I asked if they knew of anyone who was renting and if they did, to let me know. The very next moment, a woman sitting next to us apologized for interrupting, but she couldn't help overhear us and couldn't believe how serendipitous this was. Her parents' tenants were just moving out, so they had an apartment ready to be rented and it sounded like exactly what I was looking for! She gave me her number and to make a long story short, I ended up moving into that apartment by the end of that month. I didn't have to go and look at other apartments. It was so perfect. I went to the beach and came back knowing where I was living.

My parents were in shock at how quickly it happened. Ask for what you want and be open to receive the unconventional ways it may come to you.

The aim is to receive with conviction. Don't be wishy-washy about it or say, *"I shouldn't"* or, *"You shouldn't have."* Claim it. Receive it wholeheartedly and say thank you. Accept it and allow it in. When you do, an exchange takes place. There is an opportunity for you to give to the other person with your thank you! So, no, you don't have to feel guilty when receiving something or feel obligated that you now have to get them something. That's coming from scarcity and lack. Own that your genuine thank you is enough. What I want you to see is the exchange of energy that happens in giving and receiving. When someone gives from joy and overflow, they receive in the acceptance of their gift to you. Now, I'm not saying jump for joy or play it up. It's simply a heartfelt thank you. Look them in their eyes and say thank you, because they took the time out and thought of you, whether you like the gift or not. If you genuinely do not want it, say *"no, thank you."* The true essence of a gift is that someone took the time out to think of you – that's what the thank you is for.

At times, receiving big things or momentous experiences can feel overwhelming. I want you to be aware of this because I don't want you to turn down what you've been asking for out of fear of "it's happening too quickly." If this happens, I want you to pause and see all the small steps that may seem insignificant that led up to the moment of receiving the great thing or experience. Look at overwhelm as the reminder to take the appropriate time to appreciate all the hard work it took you to be in this moment. Overwhelm is asking you to make space within your body for all this goodness, not turn it away. Don't be afraid of overwhelm. Let it do its thing and allow yourself to feel all the feelings that come along with that experience. Use the tools you have to make the space within yourself to receive the good. This is expansion and you can take it. You can use your breath to move through your emotions in a healthy way. Trust that whatever situation you are in, it is the one you are meant to be in because you're in it. Trust in the invisible plan the universe has for you and walk around ready to receive.

Receiving is not something that comes naturally to most and if receiving is easy for you, celebrate that about yourself. Receiving can be a vulnerable, intimate and humbling act because with your yes you're inviting another person into your space. So, be gentle with yourself as you begin to allow yourself to expand and receive. Here's an exercise you can do to practice receiving so it becomes as natural as breathing. Allow someone to give to you. This can be anything. A compliment, a gift, a nice gesture, whatever. Allow yourself to receive that compliment by taking a moment to acknowledge the exchange that just happened. When you do, just say thank you. No explanations, apologies, or should – just thank you. A genuine "thank you" with a smile is priceless.

Giving

Giving is the magical action that allows the flow of life to function through us. Giving is the way we make space for that which we have yet to receive. Our breath is the perfect example of the harmonious relationship that exists within giving and receiving. As we exhale, we give our breath out, releasing what our bodies do not need, and making space in our lungs for the new air to come in. As we inhale, we receive our breath in, giving air to our lungs and life to our bodies. If we held our breath and didn't release, we would be closing off the flow of air and life to our bodies. If we give too much breath out without taking the breath in, we are blocking ourselves off from the energy we need to live.

This same concept applies with our money. If we hoard all our money and talents without giving them back to the world, we are cutting ourselves off to the flow of life and living from scarcity and lack. If we just give all our money and talents out without receiving compensation back for it, we'll be depleted and exhausted with life. The act of giving and receiving cannot exist without the other. They are partners, contingent on one another to exist. When we are off balance it may be that there's too much of one action going on.

Most teachings on giving have been rooted in the mindset of scarcity. For example, some of us have been taught to value ourselves on how much we give, give, and give. So much so that we don't have the energy left to give to ourselves. We sacrifice ourselves to give to others (especially caregivers), but sacrificing ourselves for the wellbeing of others has us acting from scarcity. We give so much because we have been taught we should give because it's the right thing to do – we have to, or the rules say so. "Don't be selfish!" How many times have you heard that one? These teachings are all wrong and have us giving reluctantly. This has us feeling victimized and sets the intention of resentment when giving.

I want you to see the possibility that you can be a caregiver (worker or whatever it is that is taking your time and energy) and not sacrifice yourself. You are at choice. All it requires is you coming from an abundant place where you give to yourself first, filling your cup up to overflow, therefore giving naturally from a place of joy, love, and wellbeing. You giving to yourself creates the space for others to come in and give you support because you are practicing receiving when you say "yes" to give to yourself (having boundaries will support you in creating this space for yourself). It's support that allows for sustainability. This is super important to learn and why in the Soul lesson we will talk about creating a self-care practice so you can come up with your recipe for filling yourself up because giving happens organically when we learn to give from overflow!

Imagine a cup that's under a sink of running water. What happens to the cup once it's filled? It starts to overflow and the water begins to spill over, giving to whatever is around it, naturally. The water is Source (or the universe) and the cup is our bodies. By fulfilling your internal needs with your self-care practices, you are filling your cups up (emotional body) and you begin to overflow. You are overflowing with joy, love and money, and it becomes natural – actually, necessary – for you to give. You are so full the only thing to do to relieve that feeling is to give! So, having a healthy relationship with giving allows for a balanced flow to take place.

This means when you give you do it from a place that feels good. You give because you genuinely want to and are overjoyed at the thought of giving gifts to someone else or to yourself.. When you give, it's without expectation. This is why there are times you can receive something and it feels icky. The person wasn't giving from joy or feeling good from it. It was from *"I should"* or with an expectation of receiving something back. Please, before you give, really ask yourself: Are you giving for an expectation of something in return or are you giving because it is something that feels good to do? It takes being present to the intention set behind the giving that creates the energy it is given with. One is dirty giving and the other is clean giving. I invite you to go out into the world and ask yourself the next time you are giving something: Is this clean or dirty giving?

Tool: Meditation

Meditation works similarly to your phone. Think of your phone and how it connects you to a particular person. Well, meditation is the hotline to the universe. Through meditation, you dial in to hear this wisdom and connect to your inner truth. It grounds you to the present moment so you can listen to the voice within you to show you what to do next. If you don't get an answer, wait till an answer is heard. One of my mottos is: "If you don't know what to do, then don't do anything at all, not till it's a clear yes or no." This way, you are allowing life to support you, not pushing your agenda so you can control the situation. It allows you to trust in the plan the universe has for you because you can get directions for it when you stop and get present to this very moment. The purpose of meditation is getting yourself into a state of being that has you living in the present moment (the now) and going within to tune into your internal compass.

Yes, I understand that meditation can be annoying for some people. I know, I found it super annoying when I did my seven-month-long Naam Yoga teacher training because it included meditation. If I had known ahead of time how comprehensive that training was before I joined, I never would have done it. As with most things I'm resistant to, it was worth it and life-changing. Naam Yoga is a type of yoga practice that incorporates breathwork, sound, movement and meditation, so you can be the best version of yourself. I hated, I repeat, *hated* meditating, at first! It felt like an impossible task because of how active my mind was. It's also one of the reasons why I chose the training. I knew I had to learn the tools to quiet my mind. They brought in the element of chanting, which supported me on channeling my active mind – so, singing versus thinking. This had me come up against my voice issues (I'll tell you more about that story in the Soul section) and supported me in confronting them. My point is that meditation comes in all different forms.

You don't have to be a yogi and sit in silence for an hour or chant on top of a mountain for 40 minutes a day to meditate. For me, the traditional style of meditation involving sitting in silence does not work for me. I couldn't stay consistent with it or silence my mind in this way. When I learned to do Reiki, my mind fell quiet and I was connected to a deeper wisdom and truth. I learned that all the answers I was seeking externally exist within me. So, every morning I do it gladly to ground me in my truth. Another way I connect to this wisdom is by walking out in nature. It's a moving meditation for me.

Ever go on a bike ride or a run and at a certain point your mind clears and once it does, you get answers or solutions to problems you had? That's a moving meditation and you are using the jog, walk, or bike ride (or whatever works for you) as the vehicle to get present to the now and to the present moment, because this is where all the answers live and it tunes us into our wisdom. This supply is infinite and never runs out. There are plenty of applications you can use to support you in meditating. Going back to the phone analogy – It is up to you to find the number that works best for you to dial in to the universe and this number is different for everybody. I invite you to have fun exploring the different practices that exist so you can find your magic number to the universe – and be kind to yourself as you figure out what this number is.

Below is a meditation I use with my clients to anchor into the truth of money, its abundance and harmonious flow, and to affirm its beauty of being an expression of love and gratitude. You can access the recording of this on my website, www.toniag.com/rich-resources.com.

MONEY MEDITATION

Close your eyes.
Now rub your hands together, feel the friction and heat generating between them.

Recognize this heat is energy and you are creating it.
With your eyes still closed place your hands over your heart.
Inhale and exhale deeply three times, breathing in through the nose and out through the mouth.
Breathing in all that you desire and breathing out all that no longer serves you.

Now take notice of your breath and the flow of it.

As you give breath from your body, you are making room for the next breath to enter in, allowing the flow of energy to surge through you.

A constant flow of giving and receiving. As we give, we make room to receive and as we receive, we fill ourselves up to give from overflow.

Now continue with this flow of breath and repeat silently to yourself: *"Money flows to me as easily as my breath. As I give with joy, I receive back with joy. I am in the flow of life."*

With your hands on your heart, affirm: *Money is an expression of love and a way to say thank you.*

You are grounded in abundance and anchored to the beautiful expression that money is, now open your eyes to enter this world.

———————————————

"The good news is: if you can recognize illusion as illusion, it dissolves. The recognition of illusion is also its ending. Its survival depends on your mistaking it for reality."

- Eckhart Tolle, *A New Earth*

———————————————

Soul

The topic of our souls can become super complicated when it is tied up with religion, but it isn't this crazy, scary enigma and isn't something we just experience when we are close to death. Once we learn to have an intimate relationship with ourselves and trust who we are, we come to find it's the version of ourselves that is without conditioning and is truly free. It is our inner essence, our authentic self, and the truest form of self. On this growth journey of life, we strive to merge as one with this part of ourselves, to our inner truth.

Faith is the principle we embrace as a pathway to this part of our soul to experience true bliss, joy, ecstasy and happiness. Faith is a complete trust in someone or something without any evidence of it. It gives us the courage to leap into the unknown, knowing the net is under our feet to catch us – or better yet, our wings will open at our sides, therefore allowing us to soar. We practice self-love, self-care and self-expression to connect to our faith and sound as the tools to connect us to our souls.

Self-Love

Every day I commit to myself that each step I take will be rooted in faith. It takes discipline to stay rooted in that and it's by choosing myself first and taking care of myself that I do. Yes, it's those pesky phrases: self-love and self-care. When I first heard those words, I wanted to vomit and I didn't get it at all. I thought, *"What the heck does 'self-care' mean? Take myself to the spa? Get my nails and hair done? Maybe meditate sometimes? Eat right and all of that? What about this self-love? I love myself. I work hard and go away on all these vacations!"* Of course I love myself. I don't hate myself and it's superficial thinking that something needs to be "wrong" or "negative," or "bad" for it to mean that you do not love yourself. Loving yourself is knowing that you are whole, perfect, and complete in this very moment, without a doubt.

It does not mean that there's something wrong with you or that you don't love yourself if you feel sadness or any other uncomfortable emotions. Quite the opposite. It takes courage to feel your feelings wholeheartedly. It's the repression of your emotions and avoiding your feelings that has you not loving yourself. In everyday life, most people are walking around this way and therefore operating from a place of avoidance. This is not self-serving and is likely causing you more pain. Iyanla Vanzant came up with a great acronym for pain, describing the true intention of it perfectly: *"Pay Attention Inward Now"* – PAIN.

When I first heard this acronym, I clearly saw the gift of pain and that it's your body's way of telling you to go within. Pain is not something you need to endure to prove how strong you are, it's a signpost to show you something isn't working correctly in your body: mentally, physically or intuitively. Pain is your body's messenger showing you something is off-balance. The more you resist it, the louder it gets. You can use meditation as the tool to go within and listen to what this pain has to say.

Tonia's Mini Money Message
Pain is your body's messenger
showing you something is off-balance.

When you're on an airplane, they tell you in the event of an emergency to put your oxygen mask on first, and then the mask of your child or someone else who needs help. They do this because what good are you to your child or those around you if you're passed out or even worse, dead! Every day we are walking around putting the oxygen masks on everyone else before we put it on ourselves. Having a martyr mentality is not healthy. All it creates is burnout, anger, resentment, exhaustion, stress and giving from an empty cup. If you are not taking care of yourself, this keeps you stuck in the scarcity, lack and desperation loop. Let. This. Sink. In.

If we were all operating from overflow the world would look very different. Instead of focusing on changing the world, focus on giving to yourself! Gandhi said it best: *"You must be the change you want to see in the world."* You do this by operating from overflow and giving to yourself first thing every morning. PUT YOUR OXYGEN MASK ON FIRST. Release the story or belief that it's selfish.

What's selfish is you not taking care of yourself and then going out into the world and projecting all your hurt, anger and pain on everyone else. Let. That. Sink. In. Cut that nonsense out by choosing yourself first. Loving yourself has you willing to look at the feelings you've squashed deep down inside. Looking at the situations, experiences and relationships that trigger your negative emotions. Then, with compassion for yourself, you uncover the story these emotions want to tell you and take responsibility for your actions, no longer allowing yourself to be a victim. You are inviting the hurt and the pain to come through so you can give them love and reclaim these lost parts of yourself and your power.

Kahlil Gibran says it perfectly in The Prophet: *"The deeper the sorrow carved into your being, the more joy you can contain."* The further into the dark you go, the greater the light will be on the other side. The deeper you allow yourself to experience sadness and grief, instead of repressing it, is the extent to which you can experience JOY. It's science. Look at the pendulum when it swings back and forth. The exact distance it goes from one side, it equally goes to the other. Your emotions act the same way. The more we embrace the feelings that don't feel good, the more we carve out the space for those that do.

Allowing the pendulum of your emotions to swing without judgment and with love is what creates balance within yourself. Once the pendulum loses momentum it stops in the center (it's natural place of balance). Therefore, by the law of science, it's only natural to feel all of your emotions and let the pendulum swing freely through the spectrum of your emotions. If you don't, you're robbing yourself of the experience to find balance within yourself. Give yourself permission to swing freely in experiencing all of your emotions (bad and good, sadness and happiness, grief and bliss) so that you can come out connected to your truth and in love with who you are. Perfectly, imperfect.

Self-Care

I see self-care as knowing that I am responsible for my happiness – not money, not things or anything else external to me. I am the source of my happiness. In order to operate from divine action, I chose to ground myself, every day, with my morning ritual. When I do, guidance and inspiration kicks in. When I chose not to, I operate throughout the day on auto pilot. My actions are forced and things are more difficult. I'm not in flow with life. Of course, I learned this the hard way. It took me experimenting with life to learn the recipe to make me happy. Now, I have "Tonia's Happiness Recipe" and there is a whole list of ingredients I use to sustain my happiness.

On some days I need to switch the recipe up because I'm feeling spicy. On other days I'm feeling salty, so I need the ingredients to work with the salty. It takes me being flexible and switching up the recipe when necessary. Like cooking any recipe, it takes time to perfect. You find that some spices work and others do not. Sometimes, you do the recipe exactly, but it just doesn't taste right and you realize the main ingredient was missing: love. At other times, something can no longer taste good even though it did for years and it's okay to let that go. Releasing allows the space for the new ingredient, the even tastier ingredient, to come in. As we grow, we will need new spices to support us on our journey.

Don't you see, happiness is a recipe you create for yourself! You experiment with the ingredients/tools that make your life delicious or not. Knowing what you don't like is just as important as knowing what you do. The key is to have fun discovering what your recipe is and practicing it daily. You and your happiness are worth it. Now, practicing it daily may not be a pleasant experience all the time. Every day I don't wake up happy and ready to attack my day. Far from it. Honestly most days, I say, "Screw this, I'd rather stay in bed." Happiness is simple, but not always easy. The trick is knowing that once I ground myself with my morning routine, it opens my channel to receive the messages and signs from the universe. My discipline is exercised in my morning routine because it is that simple of an act to do to be on the same wavelength to hear the universe's plan that is conspiring for all my dreams to come true.

And so, every day, my job is to ground myself so I can drop from my head to my heart and when I don't, I am intentionally choosing not to dial in to my direct line to the universe. I find that on those days, I do double the work, doubt myself, and things take longer or are harder. I realize that it would have been easier to take the five minutes out to ground myself. Happiness is simple, but choosing myself first isn't always easy. Therefore, it's not the universe "punishing me" if I don't tune into it, it just means my headphones are tuned into a different station, a station that is ran by my ego. What things can you do for yourself, first thing in the morning, to connect to the universe's hotline and your happiness?

If you are a parent or any type of caregiver, I know this can be difficult or may seem impossible to do. What makes it possible is that the timeframe of it doesn't matter. Keep in mind the KISS principle: Keep It Simple, Sexy. When you keep it simple it works, and you can build on it as time goes on, depending on what you need. Here are some suggestions you can start your day with. You can write down five things you're grateful for; these take less than five minutes to do. This has you anchoring into the energy of gratitude at the start of your day. Repeat your new money belief story from the Focus stage and your money mantra from this stage. You can do a quick five-minute meditation and use the "Headspace" application, for free, to guide you along. While you are showering, put on some music! Dance in the shower, dance while you are cooking!! Sound is the easiest tool to change your vibration because it itself is vibrational.

It's about you choosing yourself first and setting the intention that you are worth caring for. You are the only one who can give to yourself in this way. This is such an important thing to remember – especially for my caregivers out there: You can only care for others at the capacity you care for yourself. You can only receive at the capacity you receive from yourself. You can only love others at the capacity you love yourself. See the theme. The intention is to fill yourself up, first thing every day, so you go through the day in a state of overflow and abundance, putting you in a natural state of giving. So chose the thing that is simplest for you to do in the morning first. If you feel you want to do more from your happiness recipe and have more time at other parts in the day, do these extra things then.

Here is a worksheet for you to use to experiment finding your happiness recipe. I have put some suggestions on there for you to experiment with.

MY HAPPINESS RECIPE WORKSHEET

What to Do: Choose a quiet place in your home to do your morning ritual. Add your own items to the list below as things you want as part of your morning ritual.

My Recipe
- Read new money beliefs story.
- Read money mantra statement.
- Five gratitudes
- Breath work, 1-3 minutes
- *Surrender, Trust, Faith* mantra

Joy Tips:
Your morning routine or recipe is what keeps you grounded and present to The NOW. It's in the now where magic takes place and is all that truly exists. Focusing on the past creates depression and focusing on the future creates anxiety. Live in the present. It is a GIFT.

"There are 3 words that convey the secret of the art of living, the secret of all success and happiness: One With Life. Being one with life is being one with Now. You then realize that you don't live your life, but life lives you. Life is the dancer, and you are the dance."

- Eckhart Tolle, *A New Earth*

---

*To download a blank version of the my happiness recipe worksheet go to **www.toniag.com/rich-resources**

Self-Expression

When we connect our minds, bodies and souls, we live in true power, wisdom, wealth and love. Abundance is a natural by-product of this state of being. By doing our morning rituals and practicing our Happiness Recipe, we sustain happy and abundant lives. The hard work is in the discipline of using the tools we have on a daily basis to keep our vibrations high, tuned into the universe's plan and plugged into our inner wisdom versus external validation. When we do, this gives us access to our authentic form of self-expression and the courage to speak this truth. We find our true voice giving us the freedom to be who we are, wholeheartedly.

Our voices can be expressed in so many different ways: writing, journaling, singing, performing, dancing, poetry, drawing, and so much more. When we practice self-love and self-care, we access our self-expression effortlessly. This is where ease lives and simplicity reigns. I have a mighty trio that I use every morning to remind myself to keep it simple by surrendering, trusting and having faith and it takes all of fifteen seconds to do. I say ...

Surrender, Trust, Faith Mantra
"I surrender my mind.
I trust in my truth.
I have faith in my heart.
And I lead with my intuition."

While I say, "*I surrender my mind,*" I put my hands together in a prayer pose and I put them on my third eye, between my eyes. When I say, "*I trust in my truth,*" I put my hands over my throat. As

I say, "*I have faith in my heart,*" I put my hands over my heart, and as I say, "*I lead with my intuition,*" I put my hands by my pussy.

That's the formula – trust that it will happen because if it's in your mind's eye, it already is. There's nothing more to be done other than showing up, ready to receive and take action. Show up in joy, gratitude and love, like a kid on Christmas morning. Show up ready to be guided on the actions to take. When we anchor into our minds, bodies and souls through the principles of surrender, trust and faith, we have the courage to connect to our truest form of self.

In my experience, our greatest form of self-expression usually lives behind what we resist and fear most. Remember that pendulum analogy. On the other side of what we fear is what sets us free. I know it was for me. I feel freest and in my essence using my voice for speaking and writing. I had to do a lot of work to reclaim this passion and love. As a kid, I was bullied for my voice because it was deep and raspy. Boys used to tease me and say I sounded like a man. One time when I was twelve years old and at a friend's birthday party, a boy came up to me, tapped me on the shoulder and said he dedicated the song playing for me. I thought this was so sweet and felt so special. Then I listened to what song it was, "Walk Like a Man," by the Four Seasons and I felt so stupid for originally thinking the intention was sweet. This really hurt and all the years of hearing, "*I sound like a man*" scarred me. It laid down the foundation of how I saw my voice. I hated it, so I shut down and closed myself off. I never wanted to speak in public or leave voicemails on the phone. In college I never raised my hand to speak, even if I knew the answer. Public speaking equaled death and opening myself up to that pain I felt when I was bullied as a kid.

Little by little, I reclaimed my power from my fear and pain, bit by bit. I took different courses that piqued my curiosity and was right at the edge of my comfort zone. I learned to get comfortable with the uncomfortable. It's all about the small steps because before you know it, you turn around and you realize you made it up the mountain. I learned the top of one step is the bottom of another, so it is an ever-evolving process. Having patience is key and learning to enjoy the process is what makes it fun! If you're someone who is doing what you love and it's a part of your self-expression, celebrate that. That's a big deal. For anyone who is reclaiming this power for yourself, just do the next thing. Baby steps. That's how I did it and it works! So celebrate yourself on each step you take. A tool I want to share with you (that saved my life growing up) is sound and it helps you connect with the essence of your soul.

Tool: Sound

Ever listen to a song and feel it move through your whole body? Countless times, I've listened to music and gotten goose bumps in a really incredible part of the song or performance. Well, this is the power of sound. My whole life, I've used music to alter or enhance my moods. If I was sad and wanted to go deeper into that sadness, I would put on my heartbreak playlist. When I knew the time had to come to snap out of it, I would put on my motivational playlist or my happy playlist to move me out of it. Every time I put the songs on, it shifted my mood. It worked every time and so much so that my playlists are labeled by mood: happy, motivated, gym, love, heartbreak, work, piano, focus, money. It wasn't until I took the Naam Yoga course and they taught us about chanting that I learned about the transformational properties of sound.

Since sound travels at a particular frequency (the rate at which vibrations occur) it is able to alter our body's internal vibrations. Remember in the Freedom stage when we learned about the Emotional Thermometer and that our emotions carry a vibration? Well, then it makes total sense that music, a vibration, can alter our emotions, a vibration, impacting the way we feel instantly. It is the quickest way to shift our mood; it's fun and why we are learning it is as a tool today.

To this day, part of my morning routine is chanting the Triple Mantra I was taught in my yoga teacher training. It is a mantra for divine timing and protection. Chanting has healing properties because the frequency of sound synchronizes with the brainwaves and activates distress in the body. Also, when sound vibrations come in contact with the physical body, they have an effect on our consciousness at the mental (mind), emotional (body), and spiritual (soul) levels. It's the trifecta tool connecting your mind, body, and soul allowing you to access living from your inner essence and truth! Mic drop.

When it comes to sound, there are many modalities you can use to access its healing properties (chanting, sound bowl healing, drumming, etc.) and I invite you to explore them if you feel curious or called to one. For now, we will keep it simple and with something with all have access to, music. It's time to make some playlists based off your moods. If you don't feel motivated to do that, go to Spotify as they have mood playlists and they offer free accounts. Easy peasy.

I invite you to start with a money playlist for your money dates that will have you feeling excited about your money. Also, it's always good to have a happy playlist. I listen to mine most mornings when showering and getting dressed for the day, setting my intention of happy with music while having fun. Bonus joy if you sing the tunes out loud! It feels so good to use sound and make sounds. Use music to motivate you. Use sacred sound to penetrate your soul.

Congratulations on making it through the Flow stage! I am so damn proud of you. The money worksheets in this stage support you in learning about YOU and how to sustain an abundant life for yourself outside of money. If you do not learn to master yourself, you are not going to learn to master anything. Flow shows you how to free yourself from money's control by being connected to yourself on a mind, body and soul level so you are in the driver's seat of your life's journey. In the trunk, you are equipped with all the tools, when you get stuck along the way, you can just reach into your trunk and find the tool that best suits you for getting back on the road. This journey is simple, but that doesn't mean it it's always easy.

Celebrate yourself for reading through all these stages because you know a new way is possible for you and your money. The journey can be intense, the topic of money is intense, so we sprinkle it with humor and fun. This is why Fun is the next stage and uses the principles of play, curiosity, celebration and community to support you in living a life that truly ignites you and makes your heart sing with joy.

Tonia's Mini Money Life Lessons

Life Laughing at Me

The universe is laughing at me. I had today all planned and mapped out the day before. The plan was to have a great writing session today and catch up on all my writing prompts. I'll get dressed nice and early, wearing something that works for my client and the Christmas party I have after that. It's all good. Great plan.

The plan went to shit. The medicine cards I pulled today said to retreat and watch my use of power. My Divine Feminine card said for anything I do to be a Holy Hell Yes. If I'm bringing yes back, let it be a holy hell yes. I guess I didn't realize how disconnected I am today. I'm going through the motions, following the plan and getting things done, but I'm not grounded. I'm multitasking to get it all done, like painting my nails while doing a spring clean. Well, life was going to have its way with me and remind me to slow down. I went to the bathroom, annoyed that I even had to stop to pee, and the zipper on my pants broke – the whole outfit was done! Time is just buzzing by, getting closer to when I have to leave for my client, and I've done no writing and have to plan a new outfit.

Lesson: Stop forcing my agenda. I write when I am moved to write, not just because there is a group session. What I forgot is that my unbound self and cyclical self do not follow rules or order. I follow nature and the cycles of life. The cycles are telling me to slow down and breathe. Yes, yesterday was great and today is a new day. So just do what you are inspired to do versus just doing what's on the list. Now that I honor my cyclical nature, she's going to set me back on course if I'm not listening by doing silly things like my pant zipper breaking to remind me to get present! That stuff happened a lot when I was younger because I was never present in the moment and was too busy future tripping, trying to reach my future life.

I invite in spaciousness, expansion, beauty, calm, and ease. From there I access my wisdom and if it wasn't for all of my experiences, I wouldn't have the money methodology that I currently have. I can count on life to keep laughing at me and reminding me to play when I get too serious and wrapped up in the doing!! Thank you, life.

Chapter 17:
Stage Five - Fun

I find money to be a lot of fun, every little thing about it. A lot of us don't look at money in this way; most of the time, it is a pain point or we imagine it to be tons of fun, only if we had more of it. Sometimes, deep down in our psyches, we believe there is a certain burden or responsibility that comes from having "too much" money. This resistance and fear of "too much" can block us from all of life's gorgeous goodness. But have no fear, fun is here! Enjoying life outside of the context of money is actually what allows us to start having fun with our money. You start to notice that you make the fun, not money.

Ever realize the fun things in life are free? The memories you look back on or remember the most are the moments you laughed so hard you started to cry. Having a blast hanging out with your friends and loved ones, heart-warming hugs, having deep and meaningful conversations with people, dancing till you're exhausted, singing your favorite song from the top of your lungs, going for a walk in nature and so much more. The best things in life are free – money just makes things more convenient, but it does not create the experience of fun. You do by learning to unplug from the external materialistic world and plugging into your internal world where joy is. It's walking to the beat of your own drum and having a blast while you do it.

Throughout my life, I have always known the power of fun. It's how I made it through all the jobs I never really enjoyed because I was too concerned with checking off the *"I need to make money, no matter the cost"* box or really, I needed to make money to have fun. It wasn't until years later that I realized my work can be fun and something I enjoy. Regardless of where I was in life, fun has always been with me and I found it to be the secret elixir to life. Laughter, humor, pleasure, and not being so serious are what makes this journey of life an adventure and not something you are just surviving to get through or waiting till you retire to have the fun.

I invite you to look at life as a rollercoaster. Just like a rollercoaster, it is full of ups and downs, twists and turns and at times feeling as if you're flipping upside down. Anytime you begin something new, you start the climb up to your destination and it's scary going up, not seeing what's coming next. But you know the climb is bringing you to the pivotal moment, the point that you leap into the unknown and you are filled with joyful anticipation of what's to come. Then it happens, you reach the top and for that brilliant moment, it's pure bliss. Then comes the big drop and all you can do is surrender to the terror that has a pinch of excitement. Your stomach is twisting and turning, you're screaming your head off, some people have their hands up and some are grabbing the bar for dear life and it's all a rush. You go through a loop and you don't know which way is up or down. You go through twists and turns and get pushed to the left and to the right. This is what it feels like when learning something new and at the end it all levels out. It always levels out and it's pure laughter, terror and joy.

This is the journey of life. If you do not scream and release the excitement, the seriousness will eat you up whole (okay maybe not whole, but it sure will be miserable and not as fun). Allow yourself to celebrate the ups and downs of life even if at times it is scary. Don't worry, the universe has your back and will remind you to laugh at life when things are serious, just like it did with me when Jackie Chen was the driver's name in my car accident. If you still don't trust me, try it out for yourself and see. The worst thing that can happen is you're back to where you started, so no loss there. On the other hand, if you allow yourself to experiment with fun and play in your life, you just might find a new way of being that has you loving life. Allow yourself to go on a little adventure exploring play, curiosity, celebration and community to show you the way to fun. The more you play, the more money responds.

Play

I don't know which rule book said that once we reach a certain age that we shouldn't play, have fun or be silly. That's some grade A bull. Without play, life is boring and too damn serious. Life is hard enough as it is; we do not need to add to it by being miserable and taking everything so personally. If you're wondering on how to not be so serious, watch and study children. They can be upset with another child and in the next moment laughing and playing together. They do not hold a grudge or on to the hurt because they express it with a cry and then move on. They feel their emotions full out and once they do, on to the next thing. Whenever you feel you are in the thick of life, watch children play and learn from them, please. They are the teachers of unbridled joy. Their perspective on play is unmatched; the world is their playground.

Tonia's Mini Money Message
Give yourself permission to play with life.

I believe as adults we lose this sense of wonder. I remember reaching a point in my life that I didn't know what made me happy anymore and it was scary to admit that to myself. Instead of panicking or freaking out (or really, after I panicked and freaked out), I gave myself permission to play with life and it changed everything. I allowed myself to discover what makes me happy. I used money (as the tool it is) to support me in this new plan by knowing exactly what was the bare minimum amount of money I needed to live (my needs expenses number). If an activity, experience, thing, job, or person did not feel like play or bring me joy, I stopped doing it. It was my curiosity that led me on the exploration of what excites me or what fun looks like for me now. This path led me to writing this book and we will get more into that with the power of curiosity in the next section.

When you give yourself permission to play, you are choosing to have fun first, knowing that the money will follow. You have the power and authority to do this for yourself. Money flows from joy. This is why I said money loves to play. What it does is put you in a high vibration (check out the Emotional Thermometer if you forgot joy's vibration) and from there you attract all opportunities and things you desire. You give your joy to the world and it responds. This puts you in a space that you are open to receive all of life's currencies, not just money. The currencies of kindness, love, compassion, and bartering. The purpose is for you to see all of life's riches and that money is just one form of it.

The grand joke is once you stop making it about the money, you start making the money. A great tool for you to use to tap into play and happiness is with a Joy List. It's all the things and places that bring instant joy. I call these experiences my "joy spots." It's on my exploration for happiness where I created my joy list. When in the thick of sadness, worry, overwhelm or any low emotion vibration, we tend to forget there are things to raise us out of it. Instead of thinking of what to do, you just go to your joy list and do one of those things. Once you do, joy is on its way to you!

Tonia's Mini Money Message
A joy list is all the things and
places that bring you instant joy.

Your joy list is a list of activities that connect you to your joy without having to use money because as adults, the first thing we associate with having fun or play is money. It's almost as if when we get our first job, we trade our imagination for our wallets or believe we have to trade our imagination for our wallets. It's an "either or," not an "and." The story we tell ourselves is that we can't have fun because we don't have money to go on vacation or to dinner, or to the movies, or to a show – fill in whatever blank suits you. This is not what a joy list is!

When we lean on money to create joy, we become dependent on it and it takes away the use of appreciating the simple things in life or using our imagination. It's why we can get bored with life. We are expecting something or someone outside of us to spice things up, but, it's an inside job instead. Thus, we begin to practice cultivating happiness out of the simple pleasures in life and the aim is to start finding it all around you. This is what a joy list helps with. Here are some things on my joy list: being in nature in any form, beach, parks, any body of water, trees, trampolines, swings, flowers, music, castles, dancing, singing, rainbows, really big bubbles, gardens, architecture, libraries, coloring, baths – just to name a few. For me, flowers instantly snap me out of any miserable mood I'm in and they make me feel rich. They are a reminder of the beauty that exists in this world and the abundance that exists all around me right here and right now. It's instant joy for me. Going by the water is another activity. The water relaxes me. Swings in a park, another joy spot. When I swing, I'm instantly swept away from the everyday nonsense I allow to entertain my mind and enter a state of pure happiness.

Take a moment right now and create your **Joy List**. What things do you find that make you laugh, make your heart feel light, put a smile on your face, and allow your soul to feel rich? Allow yourself to play with life. It starts with just one thing and if you have more, great. If you're completely blank on what to write, don't worry, I got you. We are going to use the power of curiosity to guide you in finding joy and you can always use some of mine that I mention up above until you start exploring your joy spots.

MY JOY LIST

Joy List: These are the things that bring you joy without spending money – for example, dancing, music, nature, swings, flowers, etc.

Go out and give yourself permission to play. Allow yourself to explore in order to find the activities that bring you happiness and joy. Then write them down here.

- *Flowers*
- *Swings*
- *Dancing*

"Open your heart to those things that gave you joy as a kid. Preciousness of fantasy & imagination. Those come free …"

- Jamie Sams & David Carson

---

*To download a blank version of the my joy list go to
www.toniag.com/rich-resources

Tonia's Mini Money Life Lessons

A Walk on the Dark Side

I don't like myself. In fact, I hate myself and my life at 35. I have my own business and I don't even like what I'm doing anymore. I don't enjoy bookkeeping. Rupture, this is a complete and total rupture. I don't like what I do in my business and I no longer have a boyfriend or an apartment in the city. Bye-bye to the idea of being a wife and a mother. I don't know what happiness is for myself anymore. I have to fire myself from my own business at 35! Time to come up with a plan to cancel all my bookkeeping contracts. I'm giving myself permission to play with life and learn what makes me happy. I'm allowing myself to only do the things I love. To follow my curiosity. This is the greatest gift I can ever give myself. I have the money saved and ready to use. It's okay to give myself permission to use this money. My long-term savings account that was intended for my home, marriage or investment – not for me, but I'm the greatest investment I could put my money into. Time for the learning of me!

Tonia's Mini Money Message
I'm the greatest investment
I could put my money into.

Curiosity

"Curiosity killed the cat." Ever hear of that one? Maybe the cat died because it was so damn bored! Interesting how there are all these negative sayings around things that lead to joy. There's a reason for that, because in this world there's a prevalent mindset that it's easier to be a victim to life's circumstances than to take control of your own happiness. Well, we are breaking free of this victim mentality and universal thinking. When you don't know what you want, always follow the energy of curiosity. You either get what you want or learn what you don't – which leads to what you want anyway, resulting in a win/win. Allow yourself to experiment with life and follow the breadcrumbs. This is a motto I've used and it's yielded me so much goodness!

Tonia's Mini Money Message
"Curiosity killed the cat" or maybe the
cat died because it was so damn bored.

Following the breadcrumbs means following the signposts on the highway that the universe is giving you. These signposts can be identified by the feelings of curiosity, serendipitous moments/ experiences or butterflies in your stomach when deciding to say yes to a specific activity. There may be times that it makes absolutely no sense to do a particular activity or tie into any obvious purpose in our lives (like Naam Yoga did for me) and this can cause us to say no to it. We don't want to waste our time, money, or whatever other reason we have, but that's a mistake. Activities like these are the signposts, the breadcrumbs. Even if it is just for fun, it is worth it! Be on purpose with having fun. Also, synchronicity is a signpost that you are doing something worthwhile and in alignment with your purpose and self-expression. It's the universe's way of helping out. It's these signposts that led me to writing this book.

Here's a story to show you how following my curiosity led me to writing this book that you're reading right now, which was not something I thought I would be doing. I was told for years that I "should" write a book about money and all I know on it. I thought that was completely ridiculous. My mind said, *"I'm not smart enough, I don't know how to write well, my brother is the writer, not me, my grammar is horrible, where would I begin?"* Not too positive of a mindset on that front, but – my curiosity showed me another way was possible. It all started in 2018 when my sister goddess Nicola Humber, who I co-host the Sacred Money Circles with, opened up a publishing company (breadcrumb #1). I spoke out loud to her the terrifying words that were in my mind: *"I'll be publishing with you one day."* Who knew it would only be a year later that I would decide to write that book.

In 2019, on a road trip up to the Catskills with my good friend Adam, we were talking about life and our dreams, like we always do. It was Adam who sparked the idea of it being possible to write a book when he suggested I take all my journals and publish them, showing my personal growth process through my writing. He showed me it was easy and I had already done it (breadcrumb #2). Adam has a PhD in Psychology and is an all-round kick-ass human being who I trust, so when he mentioned this to me it really carried a lot of weight. I loved the idea and journal every day. The world makes sense to me when the pen hits the paper and I was becoming more aware of this love for writing and the breadcrumbs kept appearing.

In the summer of 2019, I was planning a trip to Italy to visit family and then to London to co-host a Sacred Money Circle workshop with Nicola. Lo and behold, when we were figuring out dates, Nicola shared that she had decided to host a writing workshop while in London. It just so happened to be on the same day I was thinking of flying over there (breadcrumb #3). How serendipitous. I recognized the synchronicity of it and did not write it off as a coincidence, and I signed up for the workshop immediately.

During the first visualization of the workshop, Nicola guided us to connect to the hidden message that needed to come through for our book. I heard "*a return to home*" and my eyes started to well up with tears as my heart started to fill with such warmth and radiant love. Me writing is a returning to home with what I instinctively love to do. It is my purpose … I am a writer, teacher and I have many books to write. The first one teaching money's methodology to the world (breadcrumb #4). The time is now and if I do not do it, then someone else will. This information has been given to me as a gift to share with the world.

So there in London, at the workshop, I mentally decided to write the book on money. It was going to be done through community and it could be a pleasurable experience because I wasn't doing it alone. I would be guided through the writing process by my dear friend Nicola. Her next Writing Mastermind was starting in September, which wasn't going to work for me because I was still in Italy. I decided I'd do the next one. Well, the universe was not having that and when I spoke to Nicola, she shared that it had been moved to the first week of October, right at the same time I would be returning home from Italy (breadcrumb #5).

While in England, my other good friend and journey partner, Mark (I'll explain more about journey partners in the last section, community), who I was meeting up with in Hastings, had planned a surprise trip for me. It was to Sissinghurst Castle Garden, I lost my mind! It was two joy spots in one. It's a castle with magical gardens created by Vita Sackville-West and her husband, Harold Nicolson. Vita Sackville-West is a famous poet and writer and her husband was an author as well (breadcrumb #6). I felt so in alignment with the energy there. Mark didn't even know about my decision to write a book. It's here at Sissinghurst that Sackville-West wrote so much of her work and received inspiration, so I shared with Mark the magic in his gift of bringing me here, the synchronicity of it and that I was writing a book. For the cherry on top, Mark's friend Maggie, who came with us to Sissinghurst Castle, is a famous author too (breadcrumb #7).

While I was sitting on the plane ready to leave London for Italy, Nicola reached out to me because it was the closing date for the Mastermind. Well, I said YES, knowing that this flight back to Italy was me saying yes to taking flight in my life. The bread-crumbs showed me the way. So, embrace the unknown and always follow your curiosity. It gives you permission to experiment with life and leads you to discover what you enjoy doing.

Framing it through the lens of experimenting is what makes it fun because doing something new can be uncomfortable, but guess what? There's nothing wrong with a little discomfort. Actually, it's a sign that it may be something you are interested in doing, but fear is blocking you by allowing perfection and failure to get in the way. Experimenting is a tool to use, to see if an activity brings you joy or not. Mistakes will happen. That's the whole point and intention; it is to learn what you do and do not like by having the courage to go and do it! Remember what I said about our self-expression: it can sometimes hide behind what we fear and resist the most. Discomfort is good. Embrace the mindset of getting comfortable with the uncomfortable. Neale Donald Walsch sums this up perfectly: *"Life begins at the end of your comfort zone."* You can't know what you don't know till you go out and learn it. Allow the feeling of curiosity to be the breadcrumb to follow and experiment with life.

I invite you to pause and take notice of some breadcrumbs you may have received along the way in your journey. Write them down, see it and acknowledge it. Recognize it as the universe conspiring for you to have all you desire. I also want you to ask yourself, is there something you've wanted to do or are curious to learn? If so, take the next step and research how and when you can do it. If nothing comes to mind, just be open to the breadcrumbs that come your way.

Celebration

There is a misconception that celebrating is just for the momentous occasions in life such as birthdays, graduations, weddings, opening a business, winning the championship, etc. These are the things "worth" celebrating and are acceptable to be visible in doing so. You ever heard of the saying, *"It's about the journey, not the destination"*? Well, this quote used to boil my blood because for a majority of my life, I was fixated on the destination, not the journey. "*Who cares about the journey,*" I thought. "*I endure and I get what I want, then I celebrate.*" Living this way made my life stressful and devoid of any internal joy. For that one day when I did get the raise or the new car, I could be happy, but for all the other days it took to get there, I wouldn't be proud of what I was doing. I would use money to give me the next fix (vacation, restaurants, bars, cloths etc.) it could buy me till I reached my next goal. Something was seriously wrong and it took me awhile to realize that.

As I made it my purpose to reclaim my happiness, I learned that it's the quiet daily wins that are worth celebrating and create sustainable joy. It's about celebrating the little things, the baby steps that leads us to our goal and vision. It's getting up and doing one thing from our happiness recipes that are worth celebrating. This is what creates daily joy and allows for us to have fun on the journey and there's nothing too small to celebrate!

The act of celebrating, which I find completely underrated, is what allows us to be comfortable with receiving the good in our lives. While working with my clients on creating their dream life, and on my journey too, I noticed an assumption about when we receive the good things in our life: there is this false perception that when a good thing comes into our life, it should feel great and not be overwhelming, but that's not true. If you haven't learned the tools to expand your capacity of feeling good and allowing yourself to receive, it can feel heavy and you can possibly sabotage the good. Celebration is one of the tools you use to process your good so it doesn't turn into a feeling of discomfort, which can cause one to reject the great experience, opportunity or thing.

You celebrate by speaking out loud the thing you've accomplished, claiming your greatness, and being vocal about the risks you've taken. At times you may not feel comfortable doing this because you're not "supposed" to boast about your accomplishments because you may make others feel bad. As Marianne Williamson says so eloquently: *"And as we let our own light shine, we unconsciously give other people permission to do the same. As we are liberated from our own fear, our presence automatically liberates others."* Celebration is the tool to shine our light. Acknowledge yourself when you do something brave, courageous and good. See your greatness; own it and claim it.

The twist is to not only shine our lights when we have the wins, but to do it when we have the failures too. We shine at all times and that means during the wins and the losses. There's so much shame surrounding failure or losing. It's such an incorrect message to teach and it's part of the illusion of fear and scarcity. Our failures are meant to be celebrated, even more so than the wins because it means we went for it! It takes courage and humility to go for something, not knowing what the end result will be. Our mistakes and failures are where our biggest lessons live. They teach us what not to do and what we don't want which then leads us to what we do want. The failures, the losses, the mistakes, they are a part of your greatness. So, celebrate them!

The other great thing about celebrating is it puts you in receptive mode. When you feel things aren't going your way or you're desiring an abundance pick me up, call a friend and have a celebration party. Toast your greatness and your mistakes. Share your courageous actions and all you've been up to. It sounds like this:

I celebrate my courage for going in front of that audience and freezing up.
I celebrate being so scared to start this money system.
I celebrate paying my bills on time.
I celebrate meditating this morning.

You celebrate yourself and you allow your friend to witness you in doing this. By allowing yourself to be seen in your celebration by speaking the words out loud, it carves space in your being to receive and gets you comfortable with that feeling of receiving. You can then switch and witness your friend as they celebrate themself. I promise you, by the end of your celebration party, you and that person will be taken higher from that experience. That is the gift of celebration; it gives you the space to digest all that is going on in your life. The wins and the losses, getting it right and making mistakes, all of it is great! So go out and find yourself a celebration partner.

It takes courage to live a life full of happiness and joy. You have this courage within you. You have a mighty heart, all of you. It is capable of moving mountains. Anything is possible. Celebrate your wins, celebrate your losses, and celebrate the journey. You are a magnificent and magical being capable of more than you know. Go out into this world, spread your wings and fly. Here is a poem I wrote when I was breaking out of the prison of perfection and fear of failure that I put myself in.

The Mighty Heart

"All these years, I was my own prisoner. Using the weapons of judgment, self-criticism and perfection. I locked myself away in a dark part of my soul and I told that little girl that she wasn't allowed to play, explore, dance, sing, or to be fully self-expressed and let that gorgeous heart of hers out to shine. It wasn't safe. People would manipulate and use the little girl. So, to keep her safe, I locked her up. I locked away my joy and creative soul. I pledged that no one would ever harm her. Little did I know that I was the very thing harming her. I became the jailer. I wouldn't allow people to see her vulnerability, which I judged as weakness. I see now the power of the mighty heart. Strength is vulnerability. I started uncovering all the lies I told myself and I grew strong. Stone by stone, the walls around me started to crumble with each lie revealed. Out of the rubble emerged a beautiful enchantress. Her wings spread wide. Her heart shone bright. She was an angel placed on this earth to spread the message of love, vulnerability and self-expression. Be who you are unapologetically. The world will adjust to your greatness."

"There is only one thing that makes a dream impossible to achieve: the fear of failure."

- Paulo Coelho

Community

In my business, I was a lone wolf for a long time. I took pride in doing things on my own to prove to others and myself how strong I was. I didn't know how to accept support and help. Receiving it was super uncomfortable and it was just easier to do everything myself, rather than letting someone else do it, have them do it wrong or not as well as I did. Well, at least that's the story I told myself, but I was getting tired of being my own cheerleader and not asking for help. When I changed that story and let support in, I experienced joy, play, fun, magic and ease in my business and life. It was incredible.

I've always known the power of support because in my personal life I've always had a strong support system with my family and friends, and it created a sense of security in my life. I recognized what a privilege it is to have this support and without it, I may not have opened my business or had the courage to go for my dreams. It gave me the strength to take risks and go for the impossible. This is why I became a coach. I give support so people can have a safe space to connect to the greatness within them, to believe in their power to risk big and go for the impossible in their lives. For everyone to have the opportunity to live their dream life and experience joy every day. It's the empowerment piece and it's my passion to empower others. What I learned is empowering others empowers the self.

Tonia's Mini Money Message
Empowering others empowers the self.

For anyone who has the opportunity to support others in pursuing their dreams, the greatest gift to receive is witnessing the moment when something that wasn't available or possible for someone before, now suddenly is. It's when a perspective shift happens, a light bulb moment. A client of mine couldn't see how she would be able to pay her bills from month to month. She was stuck in her story, "I don't make enough money to pay all my expenses." We flipped that script and I taught her to use a tool to map out her money, the balance sheet (from the Freedom stage). What she discovered is she had enough money, and even some to spare! The problem was not with her income, but with not managing the money. The best moment was when she realized this and that she was in control of her money by knowing how to manage it. She discovered something else too: she enjoyed using spreadsheets, which she previously hated! As a spreadsheet lover myself, this made my heart jump for joy. This is the power of support and community.

Support breeds possibility. Possibility becomes available when we choose to co-create with another person or multiple people. A third entity is formed when two people come together. Imagine you have two circles and a portion of the circles overlap so that they intersect with one another.

That intersection is the third entity and it's where possibility live. Your mind only knows what it knows, naturally. When you let someone else in to play with you (brainstorm), other options become available that were not there before. This other person may have the answers your mind was seeking or ask the right questions for you to seek your own answers. When you hear another person say it, you recognize it as the missing piece. The third entity. It's synergy and it's what improvisation is all about. I invite you to start improvising with life.

The larger the numbers, the greater the possibilities and ideas. Go, be a part of a community whose values, interests and intentions are in alignment with yours. A group of people who are going to raise you up, give you strength, inspire and motivate you. Yes, you can create your own community, but make sure you have communities you are a part of that hold you up as well! When you are a leader, it is easy to forget to take care of yourself because you're so busy holding space for others. It can be challenging to create the time for yourself to be taken care of. If you want to create a community, great, go for it – but also make sure you have a community that supports you in refilling your cup. The bigger the game you play, the bigger the container you want for support so you can stay giving from overflow.

If being a part of a community sounds overwhelming at first, that's okay. Baby-step your way into it. It's as simple as having one person who has your back and does not judge you; they uplift you. When you come together, you both go higher. It's a sparking and equal exchange of energy. When you feel tired or depleted, they remind you of your strength and tell you what you need to hear to move forward. It's your soul family, the people you choose. Along the way, I've had amazing people come into my soul family and my life would not be the same without them.

Where can you meet these people? Go join something you are interested in or have been curious to do. The friends I have made outside of school have all come from workshops or programs I've joined. They have been pivotal in my life's growth. I met my friend Mark when I did my yoga teacher training and ever since then, he has been my journey partner on this rollercoaster of growth and expansion. We say all the time that we might not have come as far as we have in our journeys without each other or maybe we would have, who knows. The one thing we *do* know for sure is that it wouldn't have been as fun! A "journey partner" is the term Mark and I use for our friendship together. They are someone you choose to spend your time with that supports you, with love and no judgment, in your adventure of self-discovery. They witness and listen to you as you unlearn all the conditioning that is holding you back from being your truest authentic form of self. This relationship is priceless.

We have play dates together, work dates, brainstorm ideas, movie nights, and all we want for one another is to see each other be happy and growing in our lives. That means at times saying things we may not want to hear but when it comes from love and with permission, it's okay. He & I do Reiki exchanges so we're not always just giving to ourselves and I am very fortunate as he is a gifted Reiki-Aromatherapy Practitioner. He introduced to me the fabulous essences and devas of Wisdom of the Earth that are now an integral part of my morning routine and assist me in the energy I desire to be that day. Who knew there was joy in a bottle! Well, Mark did.

Who can you have work play dates with? My friends, this journey of self-development, growth and expansion is lifelong. Having a space and/or a person who will raise your spirits up is priceless. Having support and not doing it alone is key! The natural igniting of each other's energy is what allows for the fun and the ease for this adventure called life. It's the magic of synergy. Go and grab yourself a coach, celebration partner, journey partner, create your soul family, and allow yourself to be supported by being part of a community or communities that uplift your soul. These relationships are worth more than any amount of money. It's about starting to see the value of things beyond the dollar signs.

As you are coming to the end of your money journey with this book, I want to inform you of the ways you can support yourself and create community on your next chapter with money. I invite you to create your own group to go back and complete the worksheets from this book and do the fun tips with. You make it fun by gathering one to three people who are like-minded and agree to a judgment-free zone. You then have created your own "Permission to Be Rich" group to support each other in transforming and empowering your relationship with money. If you like the idea of having a journey partner and do not know where to start, you can tune in to Mark and mines podcast, "Journey Partners," and allow us to be your journey partners in the meantime.

A great example and opportunity to witness the power of a money community is with the Sacred Money Circle workshops, which Nicola Humber and I co-created. She and I met at Mama Gena's School of Womanly Arts and did an exercise together called "Spring Cleaning" (it's a non-judgmental space to release intense emotions or "charge" on any topic, so you can be witnessed in your truth) – ever since, Nicola has been my spring cleaning partner. We did a 21-day spring clean on money and big shifts were happening in our personal lives and businesses. We recognized that there is a power and energy that is created when we are being witnessed. Things move and shift quicker. We knew we had to open up this space for others to experience this activation of abundance. We also knew to stay anchored in this energy we needed to commune consistently.

On the first Thursday of every month, Nicola and I host the Sacred Money Circle to connect to six principles of money that we learned in the first year of hosting the circles. Every time we come together in community, we affirm these principles. They are magic. It's our way of exercising our abundance muscle to keep it strong and be a beacon of abundant light in this world.

SACRED MONEY CIRCLE PRINCIPLES

1. Money isn't abundance – nature and life's experiences are.
2. Money is a form of gratitude, a way to say thank you and an expression of love.
3. Bringing all of our "too muchness" and being our fully expressed selves attracts abundance.
4. We give ourselves permission to play with life, and money responds.
5. Asking is the act of receiving.
6. We give from overflow.

"Only you can do this. Nobody can do it for you.
But if you are fortunate enough to find someone who is intensely conscious, if you can be with them, and join them in the state of presence, that can be helpful & will accelerate things. In this way, your own light will quickly grow stronger. When a log that has only just started to burn is placed next to one that is burning fiercely and after a while they are separated again, the first log will be burning with a much greater intensity. After all, it is the same fire."

- Eckhart Tolle, *The Power of Now*

A big part of the magic of the Sacred Money Circles is having a safe space to celebrate the wins and the failures when it comes to money. Money is still a very taboo topic and one of my missions is to make it mainstream. Having a safe space to do this is very important since, as we learned, it is such a vulnerable topic tied to our emotions, hence why the monthly money circles.

Also available to you is my "Permission to Be Rich" Facebook group you can join to post your ah-has, wins, failures, insights and questions on money. Last but not least, you have me. This book was my way of getting this information about money and what I teach on it out into the world, in the most accessible way possible. On my website, I have all the different ways I offer support with my programs and workshops. I am all about claiming that money pain and turning it into your money power. If you are looking for accountability and being guided more than this book, you know where to find me: www.toniag.com.

Yes, you can do this alone too, if that's what works best for you. It's all good! I celebrate you for choosing to go on this journey for yourself. I want you to know you are not alone in your money pain and that all of us, even me, experience this pain. There is no bypassing it, just learning to transmute it into your superpower. Congratulations on beginning to reclaim your money power, having a healthy harmonious relationship with it and giving yourself Permission to Be Rich.

Tonia's Mini Money Life Lessons

Back to Basics

So, we got this all wrong. Dinners, movies, being out, doing, doing, doing. These are all good and fun. But the richness, the juiciness in life, is in the stillness. It's in the quiet. It's in the void. It's lying in the arms of your lover and partner. It's kissing the head of your child. Holding them in your arms, comforting them when they fall. It's a hug from your Nonna or sitting next to her while she's cooking. Listening to her wisdom. It's sharing a laugh with your siblings. A phone call from your parents sharing the experiences of life. It's being present to the relationships in our lives and cherishing them.

It's operating from a space of overflow in our lives versus desperation. This is the key and is what's causing a big portion of pain and suffering in the world today. When we are not full, we are reactive. When we act out of desperation, our natural way of being is survival. When we are surviving, we are starving. We are starving for love, connection, quality time, wellbeing, kindness, laughter, stillness and quiet. We are starving to nurture ourselves. To stop putting ourselves second and working ourselves to death. Consumerism runs rampant in our lives, causing us to drown in debt buying things we believe will make us happy only to discover that they don't, then we rinse and repeat and move onto our next desired object. A never-ending cycle of consumerism. This is the root of our problems – society's problems, and the planet's problems.

Let's pause, take a break, and start filling up our cups of love, connection, touch, quiet, sleep and self-care. This way, we are not walking around in pain and hurting one another. We do not need to be starving. There is more than enough for us all. This desperation is a result of us not taking care of ourselves and it has us living in a scarcity mindset. We need to fill our cups so we can give from overflow because that's when abundance takes over. When we operate from this place, we know we have all that we truly need. Love, connection, quality time, wellbeing, kindness, laughter, and stillness are all free and because they are, we undervalue them.

Let's allow ourselves the gift of returning back to basics, of returning back to the simplicity of life. Let's remember that having space and time is the real luxury in life. Spaciousness. Taking up space. Sitting in silence at peace with your mind, your brain being activated by the universal Source. This is abundance, wealth, and prosperity. The richness of life exists here and now. Time to claim it.

Acknowledgements

Per le mia Nonna, grazie per aver avuto il coraggio di spostare la tua famiglia dall'Italia in America con la speranza di una vita migliore. Sono la prova che la tua speranza sta venire alla vita. Vi sarò per sempre grato per questo e per il vostro amore (To my Nonna, thank you for having the courage to move your family from Italy to America with the hopes of a better life. I am evidence of your hope coming to life. I will be forever grateful to you for this and for your love). To Mommy and Babbo, thank you for your unconditional love and support that gave me the courage to leap into my dreams. To my brother, thank you for being my partner in crime growing up with this crazy bunch. Thank you to my sister-in-law for all the laughs and being the sister, I never had. To my nephews thank you for expanding my heart and capacity to love in ways I didn't even know was possible. I love learning from the both of you.

To my Aunts, Uncles and Cousins, thank you for shaping me into the incredible, resilient, loving woman that I am today. To my friends and soul family, thank you for your love and support that reflected to me my wings so I can soar in this life. To all my family on the other side of the veil, thank you for all the love and memories and for being my angel team on the other side. I am truly blessed and looked after.

I want to thank all the people who supported me with birthing this book out into the world. To the whole Unbound Publishing Team, thank you for your guidance, patience and encouragement in this book writing journey. To my editors Emma and Jesse, thank you for making the words in my mind make sense on the pages of this book so that others can learn from it. Without you both it would just be pages of jumbled words trying to make sense. Leah, thank you for bringing the book to life with its cover and holding my hand to make all the layers of this book look pretty and fun on these pages. Thank you to the Unbound Writing Mastermind for all the unconditional love and support you've given me the many times I've hit the wall in writing this book. Nicola the words escape me in how to properly express my gratitude to you, your friendship and the impact you have made in my life. Simply, thank you goddess. This book would not have come to life without this team, so I thank you with all my heart and fiber of being.

To my early readers, Caleb, Gina, and Mark. Thank you for giving me the evidence I needed that my written word on money comes across as powerfully and supportive as my spoken word. It gave me the strength to complete this book and your feedback was invaluable in paving the way for it to be the smoothest read it could possibly be. To the Rockstar, Megan Jo Wilson thank you for helping me create the juicy title. To my love, Rich, thank you for coming into my life at just the right time. These worksheets would've been all over the place if it wasn't for your feedback and help in implementing it. I am grateful for your constant support, encouragement and for always having my back. It truly takes a village.

Resources

Recommended Reading List:

More Than a Pink Cadillac – Jim Underwood

Leading With the Heart – Mike Krzyzewski

Mama Gena's School of Womanly Arts – Regena Thomashauer

Pussy - Regena Thomashauer

The Big Leap – Gay Hendricks

The Language of Letting Go – Melody Beattie

Ask and It Is Given – Esther & Jerry Hicks

Money Is My Friend – Phil Laut

Think and Grow Rich – Napoleon Hill

The Soul of Money – Lynne Twist

E-Squared and E-Cubed – Pam Grout

Recommended Websites:

5 F's to Financial Freedom Worksheets: www.toniag.com/rich-re-sources

Rich Man Poor Man Article: https://www.cmgwealth.com/wp-content/uploads/2015/11/Rich-Man-Poor-Man-Richard-Russell-Nov-2015.pdf

Tami Coyne's website: www.tamicoyne.com

Naam Yoga's website: www.naamyogaofficial.com

World Education Foundation: www.worldef.com

Barefoot College International: www.barefootcollege.org

Red Elephant Inc: www.redelephantu.com

Belanie Dishong website: www.liveatchoice.com

Abraham Hicks: www.abraham-hicks.com

Radical Forgiveness worksheets: www.soundstrue.com/pages/radicalforgiveness

Celebration Spiritual Center website: www.celebrationsc.org

Nerdwallet.com

Bankrates.com

School of Womanly Arts: www.mamagenas.com

Mark Connolly Alchemy: www.markconnollyalchemy.com

Statistic on how much food is thrown away and wasted (Published 2017):

> https://www.nytimes.com/2017/12/12/climate/food-waste-emissions.html

Fashion Statistic:

> https://www.cnbc.com/2020/02/07/new-york-fashion-week-how-retailers-are-grappling-with-sustainability.html

About the Author

Tonia Gaudiuso aka The Money Whisperer relies on her twenty years of experience in finance and personal development to guide her clients in transforming their relationships to money. As a little girl, she knew that her superpower was organization and money management – hell, her favorite childhood toy was a cash register!

At the age of 16, Tonia took a job at a bank where she learned the value of checks and balances. She continued to work in finance while majoring in business management and minoring in psychology at Pace University. Her passion to fuse financial management and psychology would become her life's work.

After college, Tonia took a position with a title insurance company where she learned how to run a business from the ground up and soon became the Operations Manager. Still in her mid 20's, Tonia took a position as Assistant Finance Director for a non-profit where she mastered

QuickBooks, managing all accounts receivable and payable, payroll and audits. This gave Tonia hands-on experience in running a business, especially the importance of cash flow.

After leaving corporate America ten years ago, Tonia started her own business as a professional organizer. Here, she gained an up close and personal view of how people functioned and became aware of the link of how people's disorganization led to chaotic money management and how one's relationship with money was the root of that cause.

It was a light bulb moment for Tonia to redirect her business into one of a *Personal Money Expert*. She would guide clients into mastery of their own finances, a deeper understanding of their habits and the beginning of a more joyful, more grounded lifestyle. Tonia has a particular gift in supporting and guiding women to give themselves 'Permission to Be Rich.' This is her first book.

Find out more about Tonia and her work at
www.toniag.com

Money Magic Pages

Money Magic Pages

Money Magic Pages

Money Magic Pages

Money Magic Pages

CPSIA information can be obtained
at www.ICGtesting.com
Printed in the USA
BVHW092248111121
621213BV00011B/1269